DIGITAL MASQUERADE

POSTMILLENNIAL POP
General Editors: Karen Tongson and Henry Jenkins

Digital Masquerade

Feminist Rights and Queer Media in China

Jia Tan

NEW YORK UNIVERSITY PRESS

New York

NEW YORK UNIVERSITY PRESS
New York
www.nyupress.org

To protect the identities of the interviewees, the names used in this book are pseudo names, unless when the names have already been mentioned in the public domain or previously published materials. Please note that for Chinese names used in the Chinese languages or contexts, the book uses pinyin transliteration, and the surname usually comes first, followed by the given name.

Library of Congress Cataloging-in-Publication Data
Names: Tan, Jia (Professor of cultural studies), author.
Title: Digital masquerade : feminist rights and queer media in China / Jia Tan.
Description: New York : New York University Press, [2023] | Series: Postmillennial pop | Includes bibliographical references and index.
Identifiers: LCCN 2022030982 | ISBN 9781479811830 (hardback ; alk. paper) | ISBN 9781479811847 (paperback ; alk. paper) | ISBN 9781479811854 (ebook other) | ISBN 9781479811861 (ebook)
Subjects: LCSH: Feminism—China. | Internet and women—Political aspects—China. | Social media—Political aspects—China. | Sexual minorities—Political activity—China. | Mass media policy—China. | Internet policy—China.
Classification: LCC HQ1767 .T356 2023 | DDC 305.420951—dc23/eng/20220817
LC record available at https://lccn.loc.gov/2022030982

New York University Press books are printed on acid-free paper, and their binding materials are chosen for strength and durability. We strive to use environmentally responsible suppliers and materials to the greatest extent possible in publishing our books.

Manufactured in the United States of America

10 9 8 7 6 5 4 3 2 1

Also available as an ebook

To Tan Xiaochun

CONTENTS

LIST OF FIGURES

Introduction

Digital Masquerade: Assemblages and Entanglements of Gender, Sexuality, Rights, and Technology

On July 2, 2015, a few days after the US Supreme Court legalized same-sex marriage in the United States, a wedding ceremony between Li Maizi (aka Li Tingting) and her partner, who used the alias Teresa, was held in Beijing. This was one of the first public appearances of Li after she had been released from detention. A few months before, Li and four other feminists were arrested and detained for thirty-seven days in China after planning to circulate messages against sexual harassment in public spaces. Before their detention, the five feminists and their peers had been using a series of media-related activities to advocate for what they called *nüquan*, literally meaning "women's rights or power." The detention of these activists, who came to be known as the Feminist Five, sparked considerable attention at home and abroad—with Hillary Clinton speaking up on their behalf and activists around the world initiating online petitions, circulating photos, and staging street protests. Yet domestically, feminists and several others working on a variety of social issues were facing increasing state surveillance.

In Li's statement on the wedding, she expressed dissatisfaction with the institution of heterosexual marriage for how it tends to privilege men economically and legally. Nevertheless, the idea of getting married came to her when she received a postcard from Teresa during detention. On the postcard, her girlfriend suggested they get married after Li is set free. While many rights, including the right to visit and correspond with the person in the prison or detention center, are restricted to legally recognized spouses, Li saw the wedding as an occasion to advocate "equal rights" for same-sex couples. She called for legal reforms of marriage rights, adoption rights, and reproductive rights so these rights can be

Figure I.1. Journalists holding cameras at Li Maizi and Teresa's wedding. The poster on the backdrop reads, "rights feminism demands freedom, women demand same-sex marriages."

enjoyed by same-sex couples in China.[1] After the wedding, Li started the Rainbow Lawyer Group to advocate for lesbian, gay, bisexual, and transgender (LGBT) rights.[2] Li and Teresa's wedding marked one of the highlighted moments in the convergence of feminism, LGBT activism, and rights discourses. As shown in one of the event pictures (Figure I.1), the slogan on the wall reads "rights feminism demands freedom, women demand same-sex marriages." In addition to raising awareness on same-sex marriage rights in China, the event also calls for attention to the detentions of the Feminist Five and the everyday surveillance on rights feminists. The notion of rights is highly relevant in this context not only because of the reference to same-sex marriage rights but also the remark about *rights feminism* and the self-positing as rights feminists. Here, I translate *nüquan* as "rights feminism" since it is a compound term that consists of *nü* (female) and *quan* (rights). Furthermore, as I will explain later, rights feminism describes the resurgence of rights connotations in contemporary feminist practices, or a new rights feminism. Although the use of *nüquan* does not always invoke rights-related ideas, the adoption of *quan* in the naming of feminism marks a paradigmatic shift that accentuates rights-related concepts and practices.

The pictures and subsequent reports on the wedding immediately circulated on Chinese social media Weibo and WeChat. Besides creating a mini-media event on Chinese social media, the wedding was widely reported by international media such as CNN, BBC, and other regional media in Asia. It is no surprise that the event was framed as a result of activists in China being inspired by the US Supreme Court's decision to advocate the legalization of same-sex marriage. At first glance, the wedding and its media coverage may fall into the danger of projecting a narrative of progress and emancipation in terms of feminist and queer rights in which the United States represents the desirable future. The news reports cast China as a homophobic and "illiberal" place, whereas the United States is represented as the land of freedom that endorses gay rights and, thus, the destination of a queer future.

Li and Teresa's wedding resonates with the two different media representations of feminist and queer lives in China: one focuses on repressive state oppression and the control of individuals and groups, while the other highlights the emergent neoliberal trends of liberal feminism and homonormative practices. On the one hand, China is cast as illiberal and oppressive—with frequent raids of LGBT commercial venues (such as bars and clubs); the cancellation of LGBT film festivals and community events; tight surveillance of feminist and queer activists, as highlighted by the detention of the Feminist Five in 2015; and the censorship of homosexuality in films and on television and the Internet. "Illiberal" China is usually contrasted with "liberal democratic" governments in the United States, Europe, or, more recently, Taiwan or South Korea. Taiwan's legalization of same-sex marriage in 2019 made such comparison more convenient. On the other hand, pink economy has burgeoned in "neoliberal China," and liberal discourse such as equal rights for women and LGBTs have gained currency. For example, Blued is a smartphone dating app for gay men boasting of a large number of users globally. Apart from allowing users to connect with other gay men in their proximity, the app also enables users to create webcasts. Moreover, the app's parent company launched international surrogacy services in

2017.[3] Alibaba's Taobao, the online marketplace giant, launched a marketing campaign sponsoring ten gay and lesbian couples to travel to the United States to get married in 2015.[4] Alibaba's campaign illustrates what Lisa Duggan criticized as homonormativity: the politics of gay equality associated with certain privileged social groups of people who are ideal consumers in a neoliberal economy.[5] At the same time, the campaign implies what Jasbir Puar termed homonationalism: a discourse of gay and lesbian rights that supports the US missionary and rescuer discourse claiming to rescue queers from "homophobic" nations.[6]

However, the critique of neoliberal homonormativity and homonationalism, as insightful as it is, may not be sufficient to understand the complexity of feminist and queer activism in China. In another account of the aforementioned Li and Teresa's wedding, Wei Tingting, another Feminist Five activist and the host of the wedding, offered a quite different reading of the wedding. She noted that the parents and relatives from both brides' families disapproved of the wedding so much that some of them tried to stop it. Given the absence of family members at the ceremony, Wei uses *kuèr*, "queer" in Chinese, to describe the nontraditional aspects of the wedding. The wedding started with mocking remarks by Wei, who, as the host of the wedding, announced, "Marriage is like farting. You do it, and there is no need to take it seriously."[7] This humorous mocking of marriage queered the wedding ceremony and highlighted the wedding event as bodily performances. In the same article, Wei also pointed out the audience of the wedding ceremony: that around half of the guests present at the wedding were journalists, which speaks to the fact that the wedding was carefully orchestrated for social media publicity, as well as domestic and international journalistic reportage. The wedding ceremony was deliberately staged as a publicity stunt for social media and news reportage.

In fact, queer and feminist activists in China have for long creatively appropriated the rituals and symbols of the wedding ceremony. For example, He Xiaopei's nonconventional marriage or *ménage à trois* in Beijing in 2003 (Figure I.2) deliberately challenged the normative marriage, monogamy and monosexuality.[8] LGBT groups have staged samesex marriage events in the streets of Beijing and other cities since the early 2000s to increase queer visibility via news media, social media, and filmmaking. The independent documentary *New Beijing, New*

Figure I.2. Veteran filmmaker and activist He Xiaopei's unconventional wedding in 2003. Image courtesy of He Xiaopei.

Marriage (2009) documents the marriage performances of a gay couple and a lesbian couple on the street on Valentine's Day (Figure I.3).[9] Another documentary *Our Marriages: Lesbians Marry Gay Men* (2013), directed by He Xiaopei and Yuan Yuan, explores collaborative marriages between gay men and lesbian women as a tactic that negotiates with the institution of heterosexual marriage (Figure I.4). Further, women's wedding gowns splattered with fake blood were used by feminist activist groups in public performances to raise awareness of domestic violence in 2012. This action was featured on the cover of Leta Hong Fincher's book *Betraying the Big Brother*, symbolizing what she calls the "feminist awakening" in China.[10] In all these cases, wedding ceremonies or symbols are bodily performances and enactments that are entangled with notions of same-sex marriage, equal rights, and gender equality. These examples show that, for feminist and queer activists in China, marriage and its attendant rituals have more complicated implications than calling for the legalization of same-sex marriage under the framework of equal rights.

Figure 1.3. Image of the same-sex wedding ceremony performance on the street of Beijing from *New Beijing, New Marriage*. Image courtesy of Yuan Yuan.

More importantly, these bodily performances and enactments are intended to reach a broader audience through the aid of digital media. Li and Teresa's wedding, like the bloody brides, were planned to be reported on media and disseminated through social media. In earlier staging of lesbian and gay weddings on the street, the participants also consciously posed for the digital cameras and camcorders. In other words, the specificity and affordances of the media, whether photography, video, or social media, inevitably influence how these bodily performances and enactments take place.

The examples point to a rich, yet overlooked, heterogenous formation of feminist and queer activism in the digital age that encompasses a wide range of issues on rights, identity, the body, marriage, family, law, labor relations, education, and so on. This book aims to chart this heterogenous formation of a new wave of rights feminism and queer activism in contemporary China, including the convergence of feminist and queer practices—which highlights the often-neglected queer presence in the feminist movement—as well as a gendered perspective on LGBT movements in China. As political and legal reforms remain elusive, a

Figure 1.4. The movie poster of *Our Marriages: When Lesbians Marry Gay Men*. Image courtesy of He Xiaopei.

significant portion of activist practices that advocate for different kinds of rights for women and sexual minorities take digitally facilitated forms such as activist documentaries, community filmmaking, film festivals, social media advocacy, and social media community entertainment. In this book, I use terms such as LGBT or queer (*kuèr*) as they are actively adopted by the *tongzhi* movement.[11] The Chinese term *tongzhi* was first appropriated by queer people in Hong Kong and Taiwan and then circulated back to mainland China to describe homosexuals and later sexual minorities in general.[12]

As the diverse appropriation of wedding rituals illustrate, the expressions of rights—be it women's rights or LGBT rights—are oftentimes realized through bodily performances and enactments that are mediated through digital media. The digital technology is much more than a transparent backdrop of these practices. Instead, media technology such as digital filmmaking, photography, and social media play an important role, as they are essential in framing the form as well as aesthetics of feminist and queer practices. The importance of digital media points to the following questions: What is the role of digital technology in this new wave of rights feminism and queer activism? How do feminist and queer activists use digital media to engage, develop, or challenge rights-related concepts relevant to gender and sexuality? What do the terms *nüquan* (feminist), *kuèr* (queer), and *quan* (rights) actually mean when used in different contexts?

To answer these questions, I develop the notion of "digital masquerade" to theorize the entangled and co-constitutive relationship between technology and gender/sexuality/rights articulations in a specific sociohistorical context. The concept of masquerade has a long history in feminist psychoanalytic theory and film spectatorship theory. It is also used to investigate the relationship between gender and identity expressions in cultural texts. While these notions of masquerade usually presume an individualized identity concerning gender and sexuality, my deployment of the concept "digital masquerade" encapsulates the entangled relationship of digital media and feminist and queer culture, as well as the rights discourse in China. In particular, I use digital masquerade to intervene in current debates on the "liberal paradigm" and the critique of it in feminism, queer studies, and rights studies, or what I call the "liberal paradigm critique." As Li and Teresa's wedding demonstrates, the framing of China as illiberal overlooks significant social changes brought by feminist and LGBT activism, many of which rely on self-organizing and community-organizing uses of media. In the following section, I will first elaborate in detail the "liberal paradigm critique" in gender, queer, and rights studies. Specifically, I look at the tension between two approaches—the "liberal paradigm" that includes the study of rights movements with an emphasis on the usefulness of rights; and the "liberal paradigm critique" that offers new insights into gender and queer studies while questioning Eurocentric, normativized conceptions of rights. Then I will explain why the studies of rights is important for Chinese feminism and LGBT activism through contextualizing the resurgence of rights feminism and the articulation of queer rights. Furthermore, by intervening in the two aforementioned paradigms, I will explain in detail how my theorization of digital masquerade innovates the study on feminism, queerness, and rights by considering technology not as things but assemblage and entanglement.

The "Liberal Paradigm Critique" in Gender, Queer, and Rights Studies

Many have cautioned against a liberal paradigm in the study of gender and sexuality, especially by teasing out the complex relationships among feminist and queer discourse and neoliberalism. For example, Nancy Fraser argues that there is an "elective affinity" between second-wave feminism and neoliberalism.[13] The ideas and ideals of second-wave feminism came to legitimate the logics and policies of neoliberalism. In particular, Fraser observes that with the prioritization of identity politics over the struggle for economic justice during the ascent of neoliberalism, second-wave feminism's critique of culture became overemphasized while its critique of economic inequality and capitalism was obscured. Similarly, in his book *The Feeling of Kinship: Queer Liberalism and the Racialization of Intimacy*, David Eng examines the emergence of "queer liberalism": the empowerment of certain homosexual individuals in the United States through the legal protection of rights to privacy and intimacy and a growing queer consumer lifestyle.[14] Indeed, as a key concept of liberalism, the notion of rights seems to be at the center of the tension between the liberal paradigm and its critique. Here, the disapproval over the liberal paradigm, or what I call the "liberal paradigm critique," can be found across women's studies and queer studies, as well as the debates on human rights studies. In the context of this book, the liberal paradigm often takes the form of a "liberal feminist paradigm" or "liberal queer rights paradigm."

This tension between the feminist and queer rights liberal paradigm and its critique is well reflected in two approaches on human rights: namely, the studies of rights-based movements and critical human rights studies. Critical human rights studies have analyzed the problematic tendencies in the ideas of human rights, women's rights, and LGBT rights. Scholars have criticized the abstract nature of rights,[15] the tendency of the discourse of rights to subscribe to a Eurocentric and teleological view of human progress,[16] and the "militarist and imperialist instrumentalization of human-rights discourse."[17]

The promotion of women's rights has also been criticized in several ways: it buttresses the moral superiority of countries in the global North, elides the diversity of women's experience, and privileges certain groups of women as the recipients of rights;[18] it is complicit with conservative or problematic ideologies such as gender and sexual hierarchy,[19] nationalism,[20] imperialism,[21] neoliberalism,[22] and neocolonialism.[23] Similarly, normativized LGBT rights, oftentimes promoted by international non-governmental organizations (NGOs), are critiqued for supporting US missionary and savior discourse—which claims to rescue women and, more recently, queers from "uncivilized" nations.[24] Implicit in such discourse of LGBT rights is the "teleological development" narrative in queer globalization, which suggests that "non-Euro-American queerness must consciously assume the burdens of representing itself . . . as 'gay' in order to attain political consciousness, subjectivity, and global modernity."[25]

While critical human rights studies have cautioned against the unintended consequences of mobilizing the discourse of rights, the studies of rights-based feminist and queer movements, or the "feminist and queer rights liberal paradigm," investigate how activists appropriate the rights discourse in different cultural contexts and stress the usefulness and importance of the rights discourse. For example, the "rights-based approach," which combines human rights concerns and sustainable development, has become central to transnational women's activism in the new millennium.[26] For these activists, the discourse of human rights is an effective tool to lobby governments and international organizations to provide the conditions for development in the global South.[27] Similarly, studies on rights-based queer movements have shed light on the processes through which activists make the rights discourse resonate with local people. For example, in Argentina, the discourse of human rights, which has gained currency with the general public after the fall of the military regime, enables gay activists there to frame their struggle "as part and parcel of the broader democratization of the political system," so their causes appeal to a broader public.[28] Lynette Chua's study on the activists in Myanmar working on the issues of sexual orientation and gender identity also shows the usefulness of the rights discourse in mobilization.[29] To develop oppositional consciousness among gender and sexual minorities, these activists selectively adopt the norms of human rights to fit local cultural beliefs and practices as well as link the mistreatment of sexual and gender minorities to the collective suffering under the military regime. Notably, Chua argues that the use of the human rights discourse does not necessarily reproduce Western conceptions of LGBT people or erase local cultural practices. Rather, the Burmese activists flexibly use terminologies and produce new identities in different settings.[30] Taken together, these studies illustrate that rights are not static but acquire different meanings at different historical periods and in different sites.[31]

When Rights Meet Feminism and Queer Articulation in China

The "liberal paradigm critique," or critical human rights studies that caution against Eurocentric, normativized, and teleological conceptions of rights, seems to depart from the "liberal paradigm," or the studies of rights-based feminist and queer social movements that stress the usefulness and importance of the rights discourse. Yet rights-related articulations are not simply a transplant of (feminist and queer) liberalism. Historically speaking, the term *quan*, which serves as the Chinese translation of "rights," is not new in China. As Marina Svensson has argued, the concept of human rights was not imposed by foreigners but was actively adopted by the Chinese people themselves for their own ends throughout the twentieth century.[32] The term *nüquan* (women's rights), together with terms such as *renquan* (human rights) and *minquan* (people's rights), entered Chinese public discourses at the beginning of the twentieth century through Japanese translation of Western words.[33] Around the time of the Xinhai Revolution in 1911, multiple conceptions of *nüquan*, or women's rights, coexisted in Chinese public discourses, yet all these conceptions suggested that "natural rights" are rights that humans possess from birth.[34] This emphasis on "natural rights" is heavily influenced by the concept of *tianfu renquan* (natural rights), which means that everyone is born as a human, regardless of gender.[35]

Yet the notion of women's rights came under attack for its connotation of a "bourgeois" worldview during Mao's socialist period as the state-sponsored Women's Federation monopolized discourse on women.[36] Since the 1990s, *nüxing zhuyi* has served as the common term standing for feminism in Chinese.[37] Female, or *nüxing*, emphasizes a feminine identity, and the meaning of rights is obscured. The term of *nüquan* has been gaining currency since the 2000s. While Lisa Rofel has pointed out that the Chinese state's constraints on civil and human rights have resulted in a kind of LGBT political engagement that is not centered around demanding rights from the state,[38] my field research in China between 2014 and 2019 allowed me to see changes in the kind of activism analyzed by Rofel. While collecting data in that period, I noticed the frequent reference to rights-related concepts by feminist and queer activists. Several queer activists leverage different media platforms and events (such as women's and queer film festivals, as well as media campaigns) to advocate different forms of *quan* for various sexual minority groups—using terms such as *tongzhi* rights, gay rights, lesbian rights, sexual rights, LGBT rights, or transgender rights. Rights discourses are also extended in community discussions on LGBT parenthood to describe rights of reproduction for single and/or lesbian women, child custody, rights for employment, and so on. These abundant contemporary examples of women's rights, LGBT rights, sexual rights, and related concepts attest to the proliferation of *quan* discourses in concepts related to gender and sexuality. As political and legal reforms remain difficult, many of these activist practices take media-related forms such as webzines, filmmaking, or media campaigns to advocate different forms of *quan* for women and sexual minorities.

In this book, I use "rights feminism" to translate the term *nüquan* in order to describe the resurgence of *nüquan*, or women's rights, in contemporary feminist articulations. The notion of *quan* has gained increasing visibility, as feminist and queer activists leverage different media platforms and events (such as e-newspapers, e-journals, women's and queer film festivals, and media campaigns) to advocate different forms of *quan* for women and sexual minorities—using terms such as *nüquan* (women's rights), *quanli* (rights and power), *quanyi* (rights and interests), and *weiquan* (rights defense) for sexual and gender minorities. Different from the reference to women's rights in the 1990s, this new wave of rights feminism is nongovernmental and largely media-based. I use the term "new rights feminism" to highlight the new branch of feminist articulation that is appropriating the notion of rights. While the idea of rights is criticized in liberal feminist paradigm and liberal queer rights paradigm, the new rights feminism and queer *quan* practices in China provide a more complicated picture. As I will explain in this book, the expanding discourses of new rights feminism and queer *quan* can refer to a rich repertoire of rights-related practices that are situational and flexible, unofficial and pragmatic, and sometimes ambivalent and even contradictory.

What is the relationship between the re-emergence of *quan* in feminist/queer articulations and the official discourse on *quan*? The official discourse on human rights in China, exemplified by the publications affiliated with the China Society for Human Rights Studies (CSHRS), is a state-endorsed regime "with Chinese characteristics" that emphasizes collective rights instead of individual rights.[39] The official discourse also pays more attention to issues such as poverty, access to food and health, and so on. The recent emergence of *nüquan* is related to the *weiquan* (rights defense) social movement—which mainly involves struggles for labor rights, property rights, and land rights, as opposed to the universal notion of human rights.[40] It has been argued that this recent emergence of "rights talk" in China is more concerned with socioeconomic livelihood than political rights.[41] Yet a seemingly more universal understanding of rights has also emerged in the demand for social recognition for certain groups' moral status or identity.[42] The recent discourse of rights in the politics of recognition concerning women and LGBT people intervenes in the academic debate on the recent "rights talk" in China, which has largely focused on the politics of redistribution.

Queer theory as an academic field is marginalized in China, yet the discussion of the meanings of queerness and the adoption of the term *ku'er* are more common among feminist and LGBT NGOs and the activist community.[43] The rights articulations of queer activism in China is also a recent phenomenon, and the existing scholarship on queer China offers crucial insights on contemporary "neoliberal" China and queer culture. Following the critique of the limitation of the liberal paradigm in the feminist and queer discourse earlier, these studies offer important reflections on queer politics in neoliberalized China. Most notably, Lisa Rofel's influential work explores how neoliberal subjectivities are created through the production of various desires, including the emergence of gay identities and practices in post-Mao China.[44] Travis Kong's *Chinese Male Homosexualities: Memba, Tongzhi and Golden Boy* examines how the construction of "proper" gay citizenship in urban China immediately marginalizes subordinate queer transient subjects, such as rural-to-urban migrants or sex workers. Kong points out that with the emergence of a new urban homosexual subject in neoliberalized China, a complicated identity such as "rural-to-urban migrant, sex worker, or man-who-has-sex-with-man" is "constructed as a subordinate queer transient urban subject who is desperately seeking a 'proper' gay citizenship that he always fails to attain."[45] In his book *Queer Marxism in Two Chinas*, Petrus Liu astutely identifies "a liberal pluralist culture of identity politics that is distinctively American"[46] shaped by the "dematerializing tendency" in contemporary queer theory.[47] This recent turn of queer theory, according to Liu, restricts other approaches in queer and LGBT studies, such as the "queer of color critique" that is based on the intersectionality of identity categories, and the critique of the "new homonormativity" that emerged in a neoliberal context. Liu presents queer Marxism and the geopolitics of the two Chinas as a challenge to the liberal queer paradigm, which endorses "queer emancipation grounded in liberal values of privacy, tolerance, individual rights, and diversity."[48] Further, in *Queer Singapore: Illiberal Citizenship and Mediated Cultures*, Audrey Yue questions the universality of the emancipation discourse of rights and situates queer cultures of Singapore through the lens of Singapore's governance of illiberal pragmatics. The concept of illiberal pragmatics highlights the paradox in which homosexual is illegal and subject to state sanction while at the same time it is tolerated and even encouraged as affording new opportunities for economic development.[49]

Expanding on these critiques of "liberal queer paradigm" in queer studies, this book changes gears to focus on the complexity of rights feminism and LGBT rights. It is the first monograph to look at feminism and queer activism in China from the perspective of rights. Furthermore, although rights studies is a vast scholarly field, studies on rights in China have been predominately skewed towards labor disputes and legal systems, whereas studies on women's rights and LGBT rights remain relatively marginal. Specifically, this book sees feminist and queer media culture in China as *processes of digital masquerading* that articulate, generate, and contest feminist, queer, and rights-related concepts and practices to intervene in the existing critique on feminist and queer liberalism, as well as social movement studies. While several studies on liberal feminist and queer articulation, especially rights studies, have predominantly focused on the discourse of rights, this book reorients the focus to examine technologized masquerading, including what I call "performative rights," and aims to propose an entangled understanding of feminist and queer articulation, digital media, and rights.

From Feminist Masquerade to Digital Masquerade

Let me detour slightly to explain my choice of the word "masquerade." Masquerade usually refers to the wearing of masks or disguises, dresses, or costumes. It also implies pretense and deceit, passing as someone or something else, or assuming the appearance of something else. Its Latin etymologic roots trace back to "*masquarata*," later "mascaraed," or masked entertainment in French.[50] In later, psychoanalysis-influenced gender theory, masquerade is expanded to explore identity difference, passing, and drag. The ancient association of masquerade with materialistic entities such as dresses, masks, and costumes is easily forgotten as the meaning has now expanded to bodily, psychic, and social processes. Masquerade has since been theorized in a symbolic and metaphorical way. Yet, there are at least two aspects that are usually overlooked in current scholarly discussions on masquerade. First, masquerade, though oftentimes understood in the individual identitarian realm, refers to a collective gathering, or at least encompasses intersubjective interactions. Masquerade requires an audience; it could even be the self in the mirror. Second, it is the fabrics and feathers, or the materiality of the costume and mask, that constitute the actual act of masquerade. This involvement of the material culture in the act of masquerade points to the indispensable role of materiality that can be expanded to refer to the digital environment in the twenty-first century. It is these two aspects that I expand to theorize digital masquerade.

The individualized understanding of masquerade has a long history in feminist theory. To masquerade is usually understood as to pretend to be someone one is not. In her 1929 essay, "Womanliness as a Masquerade," Joan Riviere argued that femininity was a mask that women wore in order to be accepted in a male dominated world.[51] Influenced by Freud, Riviere developed masquerade as a classic feminist concept to account for sexual differences and femininity.[52] Riviere's notion of "womanliness-as-masquerade" was later discussed widely in spectatorship theory, especially the identification and the positioning of the female spectator. Laura Mulvey used the notion of spectatorial transvestism in her "Afterthoughts" on her famous article on visual pleasure and narrative cinema to explain how female viewers negotiated the problem of identifying with male characters.[53] In "Film and the Masquerade," Mary Ann Doane theorized the female spectator by using Riviere's feminine masquerade as a mechanism through which women could achieve the necessary distance from the image on screen in order to engage in film spectatorship.[54] Calling into question these psychoanalysis-informed studies on femininity and the later film spectatorship "masquerade theory," Chris Straayer points out that psychoanalytic feminist theories may run the risk of reinforcing sexism and heterosexuality, rather than accounting for the varieties of gendered and sexual identities and pleasures.[55] In contrast, Straayer rejects "the presumption that sexual difference determines different psychoanalytic positions for men and women in language, vision, and knowledge."[56] Furthermore, Straayer observes that Riviere reads her patient as "intermediate homosexual" because of "her wish for masculinity."[57] Following Freud's description of ambitious women as feminists and lesbians as masculine, Straayer suggests that Riviere's notion of masquerade has lesbian implications, which have largely been overlooked. Moreover, Straayer argues that behind the mask of femininity is not a woman but a man, as we need to overthrow the categories of essentialized "man" and "woman."[58]

Like much of the "masquerade theory" and the subsequent critiques of it, the concept of masquerade is oftentimes used to investigate the relationship between gender and identity expressions in cultural texts, including the literary tropes of mask and masquerade, filmic enactments of masculinity, drags, and feminist and queer camps. Though varied in their respective approaches to (de)construct gender and sexual differences, these notions of masquerade usually presume an individualized identity concerning gender and sexuality. The notion of masquerade is subsequently expanded to discuss other categories of identity such as race and disability.

Masquerade, with its connotations of disguise and performing, can be understood at once as both submission and disruption to the dominant social orders. As Kathleen Woodward points out, Riviere's study of "womanliness as masquerade" has introduced at least "two currently circulating notions of masquerade": one sees the inescapable female disguise "as submission to the dominant social code" while the other views "masquerade as disruptive and as resistance to patriarchal norms."[59] Passing, for example, is usually seen as a more privileged position of gender/race/ability. It is "a sign and product of assimilationist longings."[60] As pointed out by Jack Halberstam, passing "as a narrative assumes that there is a self that masquerades as another kind of self and does so successfully."[61] In contrast, drag may have the potential to "reveal the imitative structure of gender itself"[62] and subvert the conventional gender script.[63] The oscillations between the "good" masquerade and the "bad" drag are also evident in Tobin Siebers' discussion of the disability of masquerade. Siebers sees the masquerade used by people with disability "counteracts passing, claiming disability rather than concealing it." In contrast, disability drag, used by able-bodied people to play characters with disability onscreen, for example, encourages the audience to embrace disability. Yet this kind of disability drag sees disability as a "façade overlaying able-bodiedness."[64]

Cautioning against the strategic contrast among racial, gender and sexual identities, Ellen Jean Samuels challenges the claim that passing as "normal" is "by definition a form of negative disability identity."[65] Further, Samuels investigates two "invisible" identities, lesbian-femme and nonvisible disability, with an "exclusive focus on visibility as both the basis of community and the means of enacting social change."[66] As Mykel Johnson points out, "femme dykes" are not passing as straight women as they are not enacting the same "feminine" by "creating a display" of erotic beauty. They are "claiming the power" instead of being domesticated.[67] Seeing disability as masquerade, Siebers builds on Eve Sedgwick's epistemology of the closet; he argues that the closet with regard to disability and homosexuality is different, as "disability passing presents forms of legibility and illegibility that alter the logic of the closet." Siebers criticizes Riviere's framing of womanliness as "merely a symptom of internal psychic conflicts."[68] From a disability perspective, Siebers succinctly points out that the castration complex is crucial in describing the women in Riviere's notion of masquerade. This conception reflects how psychoanalysis sees all women as disabled and underlies their motives for masquerade, which are reduced to "psychological disability" of narcissism or penis envy, instead of being interpreted as political actions.[69] The blind spot within Riviere's psychoanalytic approach, for Siebers, is that "the cause of oppression usually exists in the social or built environment and not in the body."[70]

Following Siebers' point, my theorization of digital masquerade considers the technological affordance and regulatory environment in a "illiberal" context. They shape the politics of being seen and unseen, which contains yet simultaneously exceeds the body. I use masquerade to expand from the act of performing individual identities to describing the relationship between users and digital media that is shaped by both the specificity of media forms as well as regulatory forces such as censorship. The notion of digital masquerade is useful in carving out the space between institutional silencing and the "activism" of feminist, queer, and rights articulations in an authoritarian context. In her study of NGO activism in contemporary China, Jing Wang uses the term "nonconfrontational activism" to question "the universal validity of the liberal definition of 'activism,'" and "drives home the urgency of examining the agency of activists operating in authoritarian regimes."[71] Following James Scott's observation of the gap in scholarship on the "massive middle ground in which conformity is often a self-conscious strategy," Wang identifies NGO activism as China's gray zone, which operates by "taking an incremental approach to social change, staking out a politically correct position, or resorting to tactics of camouflage."[72] This idea of self-conscious non-confrontational or "camouflage" strategy that has an ambivalence about conformity is at the heart of the discussions on activism in the "illiberal" context. For example, Elisabeth Engebretsen points out that queer activism in China focuses on community work and outreach to the general public instead of "giving primacy to overt political confrontation directed at the government."[73] Similarly, in another illiberal context, Audrey Yue sees queer Singapore as operating by a "logic of queer complicity" that complicates the flows of oppositional resistance and grassroots practices.[74] Notions such as camouflage, non-confrontation, or queer complicity all signal a certain degree of self-conscious conformity. Drawing from feminist and queer theory of masquerade, the discussions on passing and invisible identities provide a new angle for looking at the presumed self-conscious conformity in framing activism in the "illiberal" contexts. The way I theorize digital masquerade goes beyond the binary of passive victims and active agents to take into account external forces, such as state sanction, and internalized self-censorship. In both cases, individuals are subjugated to normative forms of domination, whether institutionalized or psychologized heteropatriarchy.

I choose masquerade instead of other terms such as performance or staging since I would like to draw on feminist theory but also depart from it. As the term masquerade cannot be easily translated into Chinese, it also has a defamiliarizing effect that can bring about the nuances in the Chinese context beyond the liberal paradigm and its critique. Masquerade's figural references and associated embodied experience are linked to the physicality of the body. My use of masquerade departs from psychoanalytic theories and is geared towards assemblages of embodied experiences and technological affordances in specific historical contexts. Masquerade is usually understood in terms of performing femininity, which is gendered social codes. Digital masquerade does not assume there is an authentic identity of personhood behind the masquerade. Rather, digital masquerade is about the myriad ways of acting and doing *with* technology in specific contexts. Using the term masquerade also enables me to highlight the lightness, or the flexible and creative ways that digital media is used in feminist and queer activism and culture in China. Here the lightness does not only mean the portability of digital camera or mobile phone, the easy spreadablity of social media, or the fast way to connect on social apps, but also the myriad ways of creatively performing and enacting digital forms, as well as their relative light or minor presence facing the mainstream heteropatriarchy. Digital masquerade may come across as lighthearted and humorous; it may also be melancholic, heavyhearted, or filled with other dark feelings. Crossing a diverse spectrum of emotions, the term digital masquerade is productive in highlighting the lightness of digital forms, or the tactical ways of engaging technology as assemblage and entanglement.

Digital Masquerade as Assemblage and Entanglement

The study of digital technology and media has undergone a paradigmatic shift from an ontological quest in defining what is digital[75] to an investigation into how digital technology is a co-constitutive force in shaping society, especially in relation to issues such as race, class, gender, and the global division of labor.[76] Understanding the co-constitution of technology and society questions the inherent or ontological stability of certain given technologies. For example, in her book *Pressed for Time: The Acceleration of Life in Digital Capitalism*, Judy Wajcman questions the premise that temporal qualities such as instant connectivity are inherent in machines.[77] Wajcman argues that these qualities must be generated through human engagement with objects. Perceptions of time do change with new technology, but this change always occurs in the context of "pre-existing ideas, habits, material apparatuses, and cultural practices."[78] The inherent or ontological stability of technology is what Jennifer Daryl Slack and J. Macgregor Wise call "thingness," a popular understanding of technology as "stuff" and "solid, measurable things."[79] Seeing technology as "interconnectedness within which things appear, are developed, and have effects,"[80] Slack and Wise develop the framework of understanding technology as articulation and assemblage. The framework of articulation and assemblage sees that "technology is not autonomous, but is integrally connected to the context within which it is developed and used; that culture is made up of such connections; and that technologies arise within these connections as part of them and as effective within them."[81] Their use of assemblage here is drawn from Gilles Deleuze and Félix Guattari's understanding of technologies as existing "only in relation to the interminglings they make possible or that make them possible."[82] This framework of assemblage is also shared by those who highlight the co-constitution of technology and the body. For example, as Elizabeth Grosz points out, technology is what "ensures and continually refines the ongoing negotiations between bodies and things, the deepening investment of the one, the body, in the other, the thing."[83]

In her study of young migrant women's use of mobile phones in China that recognizes "the mutually constitutive nature of technology, subjectivity, and power,"[84] Cara Wallis uses "immobile mobility" to define "a socio-techno means of surpassing spatial, temporal, physical, and structural boundaries."[85] As the social space of these young female migrant workers is highly constrained by their "long working hours, rare time off, and confined social world [which] cause[s] them to be relatively immobile in the city,"[86] the notion of immobile mobility captures the complexities of their lives, as it operates via "a dual logic," in which mobile technologies can be "both liberating and constraining, and can create new opportunities for empowerment and disempowerment."[87] Specifically, Wallis sees the technology of the mobile phone as an assemblage that is made up of the articulation of "myriad socio-techno practices grounded in the material conditions of everyday life."[88] The conception as well as the empirical data of mobile phone assemblage forecloses deterministic arguments regarding technology and challenges previous works that "women are left out in relations of technology."[89]

Digital masquerade also operates the "dual logic" of resistance and disruption. Moreover, following Wallis's notion of "mobile phone assemblage," my theorization of digital masquerade goes beyond the polarized meanings of resistance/disruption and considers digital technology as assemblage and entanglement. My consideration of technology as assemblage and entanglement is also inspired by feminist epistemology that encourages us to recognize the partiality of knowledge as produced through particular subject positions and the entanglement of what is conventionally separated as subject and object.[90] Technologies are not autonomous, static artifacts. Instead, as Anne Balsamo suggests, they are manifestations of multiple interactions happening across time among "people, materialities, practices, and possibilities."[91] Notably, feminist philosopher Karen Barad's idea of "intra-action" foregrounds the relationships among the nodal points and their "entanglements."[92] Barad believes that "to be entangled is not simply to be intertwined with another, as in the joining of separate entities, but to lack an independent, self-contained existence."[93]

While my invocation of entanglement is influence by new materialism, I am also aware of Sara Ahmed's observation that previous feminist work similarly engages with "matter" and explores the "complexity of the relationship between materiality and culture."[94] Further, my deployment of entanglement is influenced by what Rey Chow calls as "the epistemic sense of entanglement," namely the "derangement in the organization of knowledge caused by unprecedented adjacency and comparability or parity"[95] in the context of globalization. In thinking about how Asia is framed transnationally, Chow envisions entanglement to be about partition and disparity rather than conjunction and similarity. My use of "entanglement" is hence influenced not only by Baradian materialism but also the postcolonial critique of the hierarchy in knowledge production. This critique of hierarchy can also be extended to include geopolitical understandings of entanglement, such as the "geopolitical, military, and epistemological entanglements" between Asia and the United States, or what Espiritu, Lowe, and Yoneyama call "transpacific entanglements" in describing the "historical and ongoing settler logics of invasion, removal, and seizure" of the American empire and militarism in Asia and the Pacific Islands.[96]

Hence, the framework of assemblage and entanglement does not entail a universal formula for deciphering technology. Rather, it recognizes technology as a particular assemblage and entanglement. In this book, I explore the entanglement between technology, gender, sexuality, and rights to offer another perspective to address the critique of liberal feminism, as well as the critique of neoliberal homonormativity and homonationalism in queer theory, and to point to its limitation in the context of "illiberal" and "neoliberal" China. As discussed earlier, these neoliberal trends that seemingly affirm marriage equality illustrate the logic of homonormativity as well as homonationalism. Intersecting feminist/LGBT media studies and studies on Chinese communication technologies, this book examines how digital technology shapes the development of feminist and queer activism in China. At the same time, it investigates how alternative media practices by sexual minorities shed light on the queering of digital technology.

Studies of feminist and LBGT media have expanded theoretical frameworks significantly in recent years. Many studies explore how digital technology has influenced the production, circulation, and consumption of feminist and lesbian, gay, bisexual, and transgender (LGBT) media in the American and European contexts.[97] The scholarship on queer Asia and media has been flourishing significantly in the last two decades.[98] Following these important works, my view of technology as assemblage and entanglement is also inspired by Kara Keeling's call for "Queer OS," or a queer operation system in which "the materiality, rhetorics, forms, and ontologies of new media readily lend themselves to a theoretical encounter with queer theory that might enliven and enrich both film and media studies and queer theory."[99] In this context, queer is not necessarily designated to describe non-normative sexualities. Rather, queer is about "naming an orientation toward various and shifting aspects of existing reality and the social norms they govern, such that it makes available pressing questions about, eccentric and/or unexpected relationships in, and possibly alternatives to those social norms."[100] My theorization of digital masquerade follows this interdisciplinary endeavor in understanding sexuality and media technologies as "mutually constitutive with" other "historical, sociocultural, conceptual phenomena that currently shape our realities" such as gender and rights articulations. In other words, my deployment of the concept of "digital masquerade" encapsulates the entangled and co-constitutive relationship between technology and feminist/queer articulations in a specific sociohistorical context.

Furthermore, the concept of digital masquerade as assemblage intervenes in the two contradictory versions of illiberal/neoliberal Chinese feminist and queer realities mentioned above, co-related with two dominant approaches in the study of Chinese digital media. These two dominant approaches are: digital authoritarianism, which stresses China's media censorship and regulation; and cyber utopianism, which emphasizes individual agency and liberation. One side of this narrative is about the utopian future, progress, convenience, individual freedom, and accessibility that are preached by multinational corporations and IT giants. Another side of this narrative is the dystopian picture of a society characterized by surveillance enabled by digital technology, where personal data is monetized for corporate uses or utilized for government monitoring and control. Research on media technologies in China also stresses technological dystopianism in "network authoritarianism"[101] or utopianism. After the Tiananmen social movement of 1989, high levels of state surveillance, the intense implementation of the Economic Reform policy, and the depoliticization of politics caused the disappearance of mass street demonstrations. In this context, a majority of the studies of online activism in China focus on actions that target specific economic needs and social justice—exploring specific issues such as labor disputes, legal injustice, corruption, and environmental pollution, as well as cyber articulations of nationalism.[102] Several studies have investigated how newer technologies have strengthened media control, surveillance, and censorship,[103] while others have examined how individuals and communities have created or reimagined social spaces via the use of the Internet and mobile communication.[104] For example, Guobin Yang's influential book *The Power of the Internet in China: Citizen Activism Online* and his subsequent works have argued for the power of the Internet in giving rise to social activism.[105] As explained in my previous discussion on masquerade, the term masquerade enables us to see practices that are at once submission and disruption to the dominant social orders. The concept of digital masquerade hence offers a way to move beyond the digital dystopia/utopia dichotomy to consider the specificities of technocultural processes. Considering feminist and queer media activism in China as digital masquerades, this book aims to move beyond the agency-conformity binary and explore digital feminist, queer, and rights articulations as assemblages of discourses, affordances, and practices.

Acts of Digital Masquerade

Attending dozens of small and large community events from 2014 to 2019, I have conducted participatory observations in bookstores, cafés, restaurants, theaters, bars, offices, activity rooms, and affordable hotels rented for company gatherings. My research has taken me to a variety of urban spaces in various cities in China. These spaces range from five-star hotels, high-end bars, and university campuses to more obscure locations such as workplaces on the outskirts of cities. Geographically, my fieldwork has brought me to major cities such as Beijing, Shanghai, Guangzhou, Shenzhen, and Chengdu, reflecting the higher concentration of feminist and queer events in urban areas. Many of these activities are attended by only a small number of people. However, I have also participated in multi-day, faith-based, or other community retreats for feminists and LGBTs that were attended by groups as large as 150 and as small as thirty. Some of the community events could reach hundreds of participants. In the larger events, I was able to meet people from across the country, including individuals from Hangzhou, Xi'an, Chongqing, Xinjiang, and also from smaller cities and towns. The content of the activities was very diverse, from feminist and queer film screenings and drama productions to art shows, from community-building events to sharing and training sessions for professionals, such as journalists, psychologists, and counselors. As someone who grew up in China and is now teaching in Hong Kong, my language and cultural experience enables me to engage in small group discussions as well as large-scale events. Drawing on semi-structured interviews with various feminist and queer media practitioners, participant observation at community events, and textual analysis of a range of digitally informed feminist and queer media (e.g., documentaries, fictional videos, film festivals, filmmaking workshops, online campaigns, and social networking mobile apps), this book is the first monograph to examines how digital technology and feminist and queer activism in China inform each other. The book is structured according to selected acts of digital masquerade. Some of these acts take the idea of masquerade more literally in their use of masking, masquerading, or performative practices, while other acts may point to the features of digital masquerade such as its lightness, or the co-constitutive relationship between digital video and queer articulations.

The most publicly visible feminist and queer activism in China in the past decade is probably the rise of new rights feminism and the associated media activism. Centering on the practices of the Youth Rights Feminist Action School before and after the detention of the Feminist Five, chapter 1 explores the entanglement of feminist action, state censorship, and social media, particularly on Weibo, a Chinese equivalent of Twitter. This chapter historicizes the emergence of new rights feminism in recent years by tracing the history of feminist media activism in China and the influence of queer feminism in the formation of new rights feminism. It highlights the overlapping histories of lesbian movements and new rights feminism movements in the emergence of rights feminists as new subjects of rights. Specifically, the role of the media in this new wave of feminist activism is understood as a form of digital masking and masquerading. This is done in three ways. First, this concept captures the self-awareness and agency of feminists who leverage the specificity of media practice to set the media agenda, increase public influence, and circumvent censorship. Second, digital masquerading refers to the digital alteration of images to tactically represent women's bodies in public spaces while circumventing censorship and possible criminalization. Masquerading highlights the figurative and corporeal dimensions in online digital activist cultures, which are often overlooked in the existing literature. Third, while in psychoanalytic theory the masquerade emphasizes individualized gendered identity, the notion of digital masquerading points to the entanglement between the medium and the subjects involved in collective efforts to organize activist actions.

Recognizing the constitutive role of the media, chapter 2 looks at the rich repertoire of *quan*—rights—in new rights feminism and LGBT activism mainly practiced by NGOs. This chapter offers a new conceptualization of *quan*, particularly the notion of performative rights, to create a dialogue between, on the one hand, the liberal paradigm critique that cautions against Eurocentric, normative, and teleological concepts of rights and, on the other, studies of rights-based feminist and queer social movements that stress the importance of rights discourse. This chapter historicizes the formation of new rights feminism and its complicated relationship with the international human rights framework by highlighting feminist activities in the 1980s. The idea of *quan*, embodied in various versions of new rights feminism and LGBT activism, was practiced through flexible and situational uses of rights, including international human rights, domestic political norms, and legal defenses of rights. These processes of rights articulation bring about what I call performative rights in which rights and media are mutually constitutive. I define performative rights as including three aspects: performative citations of rights, performative tactics of articulating rights, and media-centric rights. First, performative citations underline the appropriation of the established framework of rights that may be disruptive to conventional understandings of rights. Second, performative rights highlight the tactical, flexible, and situational use of rights in different contexts. Third, performative rights accentuate the co-constitutive role of the media.

Following the examination of gender and sexuality related NGOs in the previous chapter, chapter 3 looks at their use of the medium of digital video filmmaking as a crucial form of assemblage in which technology and queer articulations co-constitute each other. Thinking about digital filmmaking as assemblage highlights the portability and accessibility of the digital camera, as well as the ephemerality of community-based video-making workshops such as the Queer University (*ku'er daxue*) Digital Filmmaking Training Camp. In many of these queer-themed videos, multiple selves are articulated and reinvented through the construction of images and sounds. Against the backdrop of the neoliberal governance of selfhood, this new wave of community-based queer documentaries, exemplified by *Comrade Yue* (2013), embodies what I call the aesthetics of queer becoming, which expresses the more disruptive forces against the *status quo* in digital masquerading. Specifically, this chapter explores how the expressive personal histories found in these videos contest the "authentic" homosexual subjects that function as objects of knowledge in mainstream media. The bodily corporality on screen, and the intimacy of the video apparatus, operate as an interrogation of identity that intervenes in the ongoing debate between biological determinist and social constructionist views of homosexuality. Moreover, video-making itself becomes an act of coming out through testimonial, confessional, or performative modes of sound-image relationships, especially with the creative use of singing and voice-overs with accents. Here I borrow from Hamid Naficy's concept of "accented cinema"[106] and recent scholarship on queer Sinophone studies to look at accented voices in the videos. Video is a vital medium to work *through and within* the process of identification and community formation, which exemplifies the logic of assemblage and entanglement in digital masquerade.

Chapter 4 continues the discussion on digital filmmaking from the previous chapter and shifts to the exhibition of digital videos by focusing on the Asia Pacific Queer Film Festival Alliance (APQFFA), founded in 2015. Facilitated by digital communication technology, APQFFA is a network of queer film festivals held in several cities in Asia (Hong Kong, Seoul, Taipei, Tokyo, Hanoi, Mumbai, Beijing, etc.), as well as Australia, New Zealand, and Hawaiʻi. Expanding the critique of Euro-America-centrism in knowledge production, this chapter examines three spatiotemporal hierarchies through APQFFA's inter-referencing practices. First, through the analysis of the short documentary *Lady Eva* and its circulation, I look at how APQFFA opens up the issue of Pacific indigeneity in the transpacific context, which has the potential to unsettle the existing epistemic structures of queer theory that rest on the binary of West/non-West or white/Indigenous. In this way, by going beyond queer theory and China, this chapter offers a rethinking of queer practice that is useful to both area studies and Indigenous studies. Second, I investigate how APQFFA provides sites for the articulation of queer rights. Echoing the liberal paradigm critique, this chapter looks at how queer rights may perpetuate a progressivist temporal narrative based on a hierarchical arrangement of geographical places. Third, I examine how anti-institutionalism, as a practice of masquerade in the organization of the ShanghaiPRIDE Film Festival, offers a critique of gay male dominated queer film festivals and the capitalist logic that emphasizes profit and financial viability. By doing so, I scrutinize how the spatiotemporal hierarchies embedded in the film festival network complicate the understanding of inter-referencing as citation, collaboration, and competition. At the same time, I use inter-referencing to further the discussion of spatial politics in film festival studies by highlighting the spatiotemporal hierarchies.

Shifting to more commercialized forms of cultural production, chapter 5 explores lightness, the feature of digital masquerade in the "platform presentism" of video productions by two lesbian and bisexual women's social networking platforms, LESDO and the L. Moving away from the emphasis on the individual experience of spatialized intimacy and sociality of the dating app literature, this chapter looks at how lesbian dating apps produce and distribute online videos for community entertainment in China, where resources for LGBT activism are limited. Indicative of a larger convergence of video-sharing platforms and social networking platforms, the social app videos are funded by the app, feature the app in the storyline, and are intended to be watched via the app on mobile devices before being released on video-sharing sites. The social app videos are not only promotional products for the apps but also practices of discursive formation that inspire female same-sex desires and intimacy, generating new understandings of sociality among women. Despite the videos' limited focus on urban, middle-class lifestyles, a common issue observed by the liberal paradigm critique, this chapter explores how the platform presentism of the social app videos points to the platform's experimental engagement that redefines media genres and creates "light" entertainment content, thereby circumventing state censorship. The chapter also looks at how platform presentism marks a shift to lighthearted stories of the present mediated by digital platforms, which departs from previous representations of lesbianism as the mournful past.

1

Digital Masking and Masquerade

Rights Feminist Media

In June 2012, the official Weibo account of the Shanghai Subway posted a photo of a female passenger dressed in a semi-transparent dress. The caption warned, "wearing a dress like this is bound to attract sexual harassment." This post drew a cascade of criticism from female Weibo users, many of whom spoke from their personal experiences to repudiate the claim that sexual harassment is the fault of the victim. Subsequently, in the Shanghai Metro station, masked activists held a sign that read, "I can be provocative, but you can't harass me" (Figure 1.1). Shortly afterwards, the activists uploaded photos of the actions onto Weibo, which had been reposted many times and attracted a slew of commentary from the mainstream media. This was one of the first successful campaigns that started on social media and then received mainstream media attention.[1] According to the organizers, the slogan on the sign was carefully thought out to address the politics of sexual harassment.[2] "You cannot harass me" conveys the message of saying no to sexual harassment; yet the first half of the sentence, "I can be provocative," emphasizes women's liberty in wearing what they like, including sexy clothing. The whole sentence hence highlights the agency of women, instead of positioning them as victims, in the anti-sexual harassment movement. Though the use of black clothing covering the face, head, and body resonated with Muslim veil and clothing, the ethnically-Han activists were not consciously making these connections in the planning of this feminist action.[3] This lack of awareness is telling of the marginalization of Muslim issues in mainstream Chinese media, especially before anti-Muslim sentiments became more visible on Chinese social media around 2015.[4] The activists used self-made black clothing to symbolize the "restrains" on women's body, and more importantly to cover individual identity.[5] This choice of "masking" one's identity will be further contextualized later as one of

Figure 1.1. Masked activists holding signs in the public space of Shanghai's Subway. The woman on the right wears a metal bra and holds a sign that reads, "I can be provocative, but you can't harass me." Image courtesy of the participants in this event.

the features of rights feminist practices. Seen as one of earliest action of the new wave of rights feminism, this action on Shanghai Subway was soon followed by a series of other highly visible rights feminist actions in the subsequent years. In March 2015, the Feminist Five were detained for inducing social instability for their plan to circulate messages against sexual harassment in public spaces. Their detention has received considerable international attention and sparked a series of activist actions, such as online petitions, supporting photos, and street protests.[6] On the official account, the Feminist Five were detained for "disturbing public order" by planning to distribute print materials on public transportation. Although the right to protest is technically enshrined in the Constitution, public gatherings and protests are under constant surveillance and suppression. Comments on social media that are critical of the government without calling for collective action are tolerated. Those that "represent, reinforce, or spur social mobilization" offline are promptly barred by the state.[7] Despite heavy-handed censorship on Internet and mobile platforms, Chinese activists and social groups managed to express their solidarity on social media with the five after their arrest. These feminist media practices can be situated in a larger field of democratization of media usage and production in the digital age. Earlier audience studies combined textual analysis and media ethnography in studying television and popular literature,[8] whereas recent works in the field shifted their focus to participatory consumer behavior and fan activities that actively create meanings and produce content online.[9] In addition, new communication technologies, especially social media, have been playing an unprecedentedly crucial role in social movements through citizen journalism, alternative media production, etc.[10]

Social media provides the agency for social change on the one hand[11] yet undermines individual influence and curtails collective engagement on the other.[12] Current studies of Chinese social media present both optimistic and critical stances, which align with the two dominant approaches to digital Chinese media I analyzed in the introductory chapter. The first approach of digital authoritarianism stresses China's media censorship and regulation; the second approach to cyber utopianism emphasizes individual agency and liberation. Weibo, also known as microblog, remains the most influential social media in China as a result of the national ban on foreign equivalents such as Facebook and Twitter. Scholars have looked at the censorship of Weibo, including its keyword blocking,[13] paid human censor,[14] and computation manipulation of information using algorithms.[15] Jonathan Hassid argues that Weibo poses no apparent threat to the system since its users are more likely to discuss entertainment than politics or social issues.[16] The government used the platform for surveillance—public opinions and sentiments are gathered, and local government officials are monitored and penalized for malfeasance, without instituting systemic reform. Government departments, especially police and security departments, have set up Weibo accounts.[17]

On the other hand, many have noted that seemingly apolitical incidents surrounding gaming can be appropriated for political purposes,[18] and microblogs can be seen as "counter-hegemonic" practices in everyday life. Netizens (Internet citizens) voice their demand for political reform on Weibo.[19] They express public opinions on microblogs pressuring the government to reverse decisions; they also mistrust the government and dismantle the hegemonic consent.[20] In other words, Weibo loosens up government control over information spread, and the Internet is "a catalyst for social and political transformation."[21] These studies explore Weibo's potential to transform existing power structures of mainstream media and government and business elites, or to challenge the rule of the government.

Almost all of these studies, both pessimistic and optimistic, conceptualize power in terms of state and economic power, in relation to which Weibo is a tool to monitor and expose malfeasance. Identity politics and politics of recognition on Weibo are less discussed, with a few exceptions such as Uyghur media practices.[22] The ubiquitous control-resistance dichotomy in the discussion about censorship has failed to address the gendered aspect of discursive formation and the decades of growth in feminist media practices. Misogyny and stereotypical understandings of gender, including gender-based harassment and shaming, are often reinforced in the guise of behaviors "resistant" to state censorship online.[23] As I explain in the introductory chapter, studies of feminist and LBGT media have expanded theoretical frameworks significantly in recent years. Many have explored how digital technology has influenced the production, circulation, and consumption of feminist and queer media in the American, European, and Asian contexts. In recent years, the scholarship on feminist media has been blossoming. For example, Jun Li and Xiaoqin Li have looked at how media serves as a "core political resource" for young feminist movements in China, and how the young feminists' relationship with the state departs from that of earlier generations of feminists.[24] Bin Wang and Catherine Driscoll highlight the importance of social media in contemporary Chinese feminist activism and youth activism.[25] Lixian Hou looks at how young women's digital activism rewrites "the personal is political" by politicizing women's private matters for provoking public discussions.[26]

This chapter focuses on the feminist media practices before and after the detention of the Feminist Five to shed light on the dynamics between state surveillance and censorship, media activism, and feminist politics in China. Specifically, it highlights how feminist activism, exemplified by the practices of the Youth Rights Feminist Action School, creatively engages the media through the notion of "digital masking" as a mode of digital masquerade. As I explained in the introductory chapter, masquerade does not simply refer to the performance of gender but also the construction, delineation, and alteration of bodily images online. The following section will briefly outline previous feminist activism in China and its overlapping practices in relation to media, starting from the 1980s. It will also trace the influence of queer feminism in the formation of new rights feminism. It will then turn to the Youth Rights Feminist Action School, which emerged in the 2010s, and its sophisticated use of social media. The notion of digital masking and masquerade pinpoints the characteristics of the new wave of feminist media activism in China.

New Subjects of Rights: From Non-Governmental Engagement to New Rights Feminism

In socialist China under Mao's reign, official discourse supported gender equality and the liberation of women through integrating women into the workforce to build a progressive and modern nation. This version of state-sponsored feminism was criticized for overemphasizing class struggle while obscuring the structural and everyday inequalities faced by women.[27] The economic reform led by Deng Xiaoping in the late 1970s introduced a shift in gender politics by way of market liberalization. As Rofel argues, traces of neoliberalism during the reform era called for the expression of "natural" desire and gendered selfhood, which were believed to have been suppressed by socialist policies during Mao's era.[28] The cultural imperative of self-expression and the interest in gender identity lent support to the commodification of women's bodies. The portrayal of women on media diverged from the sexless and androgynous in the Cultural Revolution era, to the economically successful, consumerism-friendly, feminine, and sexually attractive.[29] The binaristic conception of traditional gender roles, which subsided in Mao's era, resurfaced during the market reform.[30]

In response to these social changes, the women's movement in the economic reform era of the 1980s and the 1990s actively involved both NGOs and state institutions.[31] The incorporation of the national Anti-Domestic Violence Network into the organizational infrastructure of the All China Women's Federation (ACWF), a state-sponsored institution tackling women's issues, was a successful example of Chinese feminists' "dual approach."[32] Unlike many feminists in the Euro-American contexts, Chinese feminists worried that an NGO's explicit oppositional stance to the state might lead to suppression, which would then compromise their ability to advocate for women. They recognized collaborating with the party-state/ACWF to be necessary for channeling their efforts into policy and legal changes.[33] This non-confrontational coexistence of state initiatives and NGOs was observed by other scholars as feminist activism in this period "simultaneously [drew] upon the political and financial resources of the state/ACWF, and [worked] on new, local initiatives."[34]

The "non-governmental" feminist engagements began in the mid-1980s and were heightened by the United Nations Fourth World Conference on Women held in Beijing in 1995. These engagements covered a wide range of women's issues, from economic and legal justice to religion and sexuality.[35] The media sector (including the press, television, and film) was becoming more commercialized in practice, but was still under the government's watch. As the media permeated people's daily lives, it became a key area of feminist study, and a powerful tool of feminist activism. Feminists in China have been monitoring the mainstream representation of gender constantly. For instance, their content analysis of news reports on domestic violence in Zhongguo Funü Bao (China Women's News) from 1984 to 2003 showed that the newspaper's typical reportage personalizes domestic violence and overlooks structural and social inequality.[36] Moreover, girls' issues have little media visibility, as they are often blended with women's issues or children's issues. Girls are usually depicted as passive victims or receivers of assistance and are rarely given an active voice.[37]

In the age of digital media, feminist media practices include the production of digital video, multimedia performance, and art installations, among others. Easier access to digital technologies, such as digital cameras, facilitates the creation of public culture.[38] Veteran feminist Ai Xiaoming has been using digital video for social engagement for decades, and she represents what Zeng Jinyan has called the "citizen intelligentsia" in China.[39] She sees her documentaries as "part of China's fledgling rights defense movement."[40] Film scholar Zhang Zhen argues that Ai's digital video activist documentaries construct a "digital political mimesis" by leveraging the accessibility of digital technologies and the Internet to mobilize the audience for social change.[41] Zhang sees Ai's documentaries as demonstrations of Jane Gaines's idea of the "pathos of facts."[42] For example, instead of aiming for journalistic reportage or projecting detached objectivity, Ai inserts herself and her camera into the scene of protest and is unabashed about her agenda. By showing that she is attacked along with other protesters, her documentary dissolves the subject-object divide. The evidence of injustice elicits "pathos"—affective, bodily responses—from the viewers, prompting them to take action for social change.[43]

The Internet aids feminist activism in China in other practices. Media Monitor for Women Network in Beijing was founded in 1996 to promote women's communication rights and gender equality in the media. In 2009, the network started to publish the weekly e-paper *Women's Voice* and launched the website of the Network. *Women's Voice* comments on current events related to women's rights and gender equality, responds to women's/gender issues reported by the mass media, reports on the work of NGOs serving women, and introduces the development of the international women's movement. The New Media Female Network (NMFN) (*xinmeiti nüxing wangluo*, also known as Women Awakening) focuses on gender issues in mass communication. Through organizing exhibitions, seminars, lectures, and journalist workshops about feminism in the Pearl River Delta region, NMFN educates the public and trains journalists to evaluate and monitor the media from a gender perspective. NMFN sees the organization of these activist events in physical spaces such as libraries and cafes as a way to reclaim the male dominated public space.[44]

This new era of feminist activism saw the emergence of the Youth Rights Feminist Action School (hereafter YRFAS) (*qingnian nüquan xingdongpai*), whose actions started to receive attention from mainstream newspapers in Beijing and Guangzhou circa 2012. YRFAS is not the designation of an organization or the exclusive title of a particular group of people. Instead, it puts a name to a form of activism in China that people recognize and a set of values that anyone can espouse. According to Lü Pin, one of the prominent feminists closely associated with YRFAS, this wave of rights feminism movement are led by a younger generation of action-oriented feminists who leverage various platforms of communication to achieve their objectives and promote an all-inclusive feminism, including some rights-based demands.[45] While previous generations of Chinese feminist activists were often intellectuals who maintained good relationships with the mainstream media—which oftentimes helped promote NGO activities with feminist messages[46]—YRFAS is made up of a younger generation of media-savvy feminists who publicize their actions and messages through social media, especially Sina Weibo, the Chinese equivalent of Twitter. For example, the Sina Weibo accounts of the two aforementioned feminist websites, namely @FeministVoices and @WomenAwakening, are run by rights feminists.[47]

Though feminists' earlier media-based practices such as activist film-making and organizations such as Media Monitor for Women Network have all addressed rights-related issues, the deliberate adaption of *nüquan*, or rights feminism, in labeling themselves and their actions is a relatively new phenomenon and marks a new height of rights consciousness. Those who were involved in earlier feminist movements or articulate feminist ideas may not necessarily identify as "feminist." One of the founders of the academic discipline of women's studies in China, Li Xiaojiang, refused to be labeled as a "feminist" when she was traveling to the United States in the 1980s.[48] According to the research by Dongchao Min in the 1990s, feminism was translated into *nvxing zhuyi*, which "emphasize[s] gender differences rather than women's rights."[49] While the translation of *nvxing zhuyi* was embraced by female intellectuals such as Zhang Jinyuan and Dai Jinhua, the same intellectuals, together with other renowned female writers, filmmakers, and public intellectuals oftentimes felt uneasy being identified as feminists or describing themselves as such in public.[50] In the next chapter, I will explore in-depth the historical contexts of the disidentification as feminist when I look into varied rights-related practices.

As explained in the introductory chapter, I translate *nüquan* as "rights feminism" to describe the appropriation of rights frameworks in the recent rise in feminist consciousness epitomized by the use of the term *nüquan* (women's rights). The rise or resurgence of *nüquan* in popular discourse has been one of the most significant rights-related phenomena since the 2000s. The high visibility of the YRFAS certainly contributed to such popularity. While the term has been used to refer to feminism in general, the term rights feminism does not always invoke meanings related to women's rights. As *quan* could also mean power, *nüquan* could also refer to empowered female individuals and the empowerment of women in general, which may not have a direct relationship to the notion of rights. Yet I use the term rights feminism to highlight this new development and the stream of feminist articulation related to the rights framework. The rights framework refers to a rich repertoire of international human rights concepts, domestic political norms, and rhetoric related to rights, legal activism, and rights defense. As the latest development of women's rights movement, this wave of rights feminism revitalizes the international women's rights framework introduced to China in the 1995 World Women's Conference in Beijing. Furthermore, I am using new rights feminism to specify this new mode of organizing nongovernmental feminist activism that emerged in the new millennium, while at the same time acknowledging the existing history of rights feminism. This articulation of new rights feminism brings about new subjects of rights claims: the rights feminists (*nüquan zhuyizhe*). The new rights feminism is closely related to the articulation of a rights feminist identity, as well as the groups and communities formed under this label.

Convergences of New Rights Feminism and Queer Feminism

Besides the development from earlier non-governmental feminist engagement to recent rights feminist media activism, another less discussed influence that contributes to the rise of rights feminism is the formation of queer feminism and social movement. Unlike the split of the lesbian movement from a larger women's movement in other cultural contexts, more dynamic and complicated cross-fertilizations took place between women's movements and lesbian movements in China. For example, the aforementioned high-impact rights feminist performances on Shanghai Subway in 2012 were organized by queer feminist activists with years of involvement in the *lala* movement.[51]

The lesbian social movement, colloquially known as the *lala* movement, provides organizational methods and discursive resources to the rights feminists. Some activists have suggested that *lala* activism predates rights feminist activism. Though women's rights have a much longer discursive history, veteran queer activist Xiaoyan points out that the "lesbian movement developed earlier than the rights feminism movement."[52] *Lala* chatrooms, forums, and independent websites started to emerge at the turn of the millennium. The 2000s have seen a rapid development of the lesbian movement, blossoming with grassroots *lala* organizations and communities nationwide. Among them are Common Language, founded in 2005 in Beijing, and *Les+*, the first *lala* magazine in China, which started publishing the same year. In the years that followed, local *lala* communities grew significantly in different parts of China. Common Language released the oral history of the *lala* community in Beijing, tracing the development of *lala* salons, lesbian bars, and other spaces. Lucetta Kam's book *Shanghai Lalas* paints a detailed picture of *lala* community formations in Shanghai in the 2010s.[53] In 2007, the founding of the Chinese Lala Alliance expanded the *lala* movement by facilitating transregional and transnational flows of people and ideas. Experienced lesbian, bisexual, and transgender activists from Hong Kong, Taiwan, and overseas lent support to the growth of these *lala* communities, introducing ideas and sharing localized activist knowledge through venues such as Lala Camp. Lala Camp was a Chinese-speaking annual training camp for organizers of local *lala* communities. It made possible the mobilization of lesbians and queer women over the country and expanded the pool of participants from major urban areas to village towns and smaller-scale cities. Many active rights feminists used to be participants of the Lala Camp. The blossoming of the *lala* movement led to a distinctive development of "Chinese queer feminism," in which queer feminists debated gay male activists and their biological essentialist views.[54]

In 2009, a street performance of two women in wedding dresses and two men in wedding dresses took place in Beijing to raise the awareness of same-sex marriages. Around the same time, rights feminists started to adopt the format of street performance and prompted their actions through media. It made such an impact that 2012 was seen as the Year of Rights Feminism. In this sense, the lesbian movement contributed to the later emergence of the new rights feminism. To see the *lala* movement as preceding the new rights feminism movement may seem counterintuitive, given the much longer history of the women's movement in China. However, the *lala* social movement inspired and lent support to the new wave of rights feminism, NGOs, and the mobilization of people. My use of the term new rights feminism underlines this specific formation of feminism influenced by queer and lesbian activism.

During my community observations, it is common to see how feminists' concerns and queer women's concerns converge and also diverge. Chinese *Vagina Monologues* theater performances, for example, started as community-created stories of female life experiences. Subsequently, monologues from queer and gender variant perspectives played by Whiskey Chow and others were also incorporated.[55] The L, the Shanghai-based lesbian dating app, whose practices I will explore more in chapter 5, served as event sponsor for Women in Tech in 2017. Due to the marginality of queer and lesbian identities in China and the predominantly patriarchal culture, many self-identified queer women are also active rights feminists. For example, Datu, one of the Feminist Five and a self-identified rights feminist who had experience in both the feminist movement and the gay and lesbian movement, or *tongzhi* movement, related:

> When I used to work in the *tongzhi* movement, I insisted that I am a straight woman who has a boyfriend. . . . After one year's activism and thoughts (after joining the rights feminism movement), I started to gradually think about myself as queer and also use lesbian as my political identity. . . . When I thought of myself as a pure "straight woman," I was found in a binary system of gender identity and sexual orientation. I feel there is a lack of possibility in my life. . . . Rights feminism itself guarantees the rights of homosexuals. . . . My body and spirit have felt liberation and freedom that I have never felt before.[56]

Datu's experience vividly illustrates the cross-fertilization between new rights feminism and the queer movement. Besides the overlap of people, activities, and ideas between feminist and queer activism in the Chinese context, putting feminism in dialogue with queer thinking and lesbian movements has larger theoretical ramifications. It expands the historiography of feminism in China, which oftentimes sidelines lesbians and female homoeroticism. This marginalization of the lesbian experience is an ongoing struggle. Veteran queer activist Xiaoyan pointed out the invisibility of lesbian activists, or the absence of *lala* subjectivity, in rights feminism movements. This absence could have derived from the feminists' strategic considerations as well as neglect by external forces. When Xiaoyan expressed her view to several feminist activists, these activists recognized the importance of the demands of lesbians. Yet they could not seem to find a suitable place to voice lesbian concerns in feminist movements. The conversations between Xiaoyan and the feminist activists were interrupted by another veteran feminist: "It is very good to express feminist demands, but there shouldn't be an emphasis on the *lala* identity, [for] this will make the public misunderstand feminism. Also, this kind of minority concern shouldn't be over-emphasized."[57] This point of view, which marginalizes lesbian concerns in feminist movements, is consistent with my interview with feminists who are actively involved in the movement but who think "LGBT is another field when compared to feminism."[58] Yet the overlapping histories of lesbian movements and new rights feminism movements tell us otherwise and demonstrate the presence of the *lala* movement in forming the wave of rights feminism. Though the term rights feminism has a much longer history in China, it is fair to say that the *lala* movement predates the new rights feminism and contributes to the development of the latter. Moreover, the entangled history between queer feminism and rights feminism points to what Marjorie Garber calls a "category crisis"[59] between "heterosexual women" and "queer women." This is also why my book looks at feminist and queer media activism at the same time. After contextualizing the emergence of rights feminist media activism, in the following sections, I examine how media-based practices exemplify what I call digital masking and masquerade, a new form of construction, delineation, and alteration of bodily images online for activist ends.

Masking, Masquerade, and Censorship on Weibo

To masquerade is usually understood as to pretend to be someone one is not. The concept of masquerade is oftentimes used to discuss the relationship between gender and identity expressions in cultural texts. They range from the literary tropes of masks and masquerade to filmic enactments of masculinity.[60] As I explain in the introduction, masquerade suggests the inescapable female disguise is submissive to the dominant social code on the one hand, and disruptive and resistant to patriarchal norms on the other.[61] The practices of Chinese rights feminists present a complicated picture beyond the two polarized understandings of masquerade. I use masquerade to expand from the act of performing gender to describing a new relationship between users and digital media that is resistant to patriarchy and conditioned by both state censorship and the specificity of media forms. The notion of digital masquerade captures how feminists use media tactically and set their agenda carefully. Their actions demonstrate a high level of self-awareness of possible criminalization and strong agency that negotiates with strict state surveillance. In particular, digital masking is one of the masquerade tactics used to intervene in public spaces and voice concerns.

To masquerade—masked or unmasked—is to pose for the camera, the journalist, and ultimately the reader of the news or the Internet user. Compared to the previous generation of feminists who focused on critiquing media representation, the rights feminists are news creators who set the agenda on both traditional media (print and television) and online media. In the early stage, YRFAS and other associated feminists, including queer feminists, deliberately took to the street in order to attract the attention of mainstream media. Later on, feminists, no longer relying on mainstream news media as the main outlet, have leveraged social media to generate social impacts. The heated discussion online triggered by rights feminists about a particular event would be noticed and then reported by mainstream news media.

The use of masks in this wave of YRFAS actions deserves further theorization. The groundbreaking performance in Shanghai Subway, mentioned in the beginning of this chapter, is a good example of the use of masking tactics. One of activists is wearing a black headscarf and mask, and at the same time a metal bra and short skirt. Masks have multilayered gendered and racialized meanings. During the severe acute respiratory syndrome (SARS) outbreak in 2003, surgical masks marked Asian bodies as "unmistakable signs of racial difference," a phenomenon observed again during the early days of the COVID-19 pandemic. According to Thy Phu, masks and their "paradoxically legible anonymity" perpetuate the "Yellow Peril hysteria," a discourse of Asians and Asian Americans that recodifies the mask as "a multilayered signifying system."[62] Masking has a long tradition in feminist art. For example, the gorilla masks adopted by the American artist collective Guerrilla Girls channel collective concerns under anonymity. The use of masks is significant as they display "maskulinity," a term coined by founding member Käthe Kollwitz in an interview in 1995, to challenge the dominance of white male authorship in the art world.[63] At the same time, masking tactics are criticized for essentializing women or reinforcing "tokenism or faux-membership"[64] as they gloss over their collective's ever-growing and perpetually changing racial, gender, and social diversity.[65] However, in her reading of the masking tactics used by the Russian feminist activist group Pussy Riot, Rosi Braidotti points out that the potential of masking exceeds the limits of identity politics.[66] For Braidotti, instead of essentializing women, masked faces of Pussy Riot are at once "over-exposed celebrities and anonymous militants" that position their "temporary identity claims strategically" in order to activate processes of "multiple becomings" against the rule of commodification.[67]

In the context of the above-mentioned display of the slogan on Shanghai Subway in the beginning of this chapter, the covering of faces or masking tactics can be used to avoid possible online trolling and misogynist attacks after the images were posted online. However, the activists involved stated that censorship and cyberbullying were not the main concerns behind the decision of masking. Rather, the conscious decision to cover one's face is an effort to make a collective, instead of an individual, demand in public. This emphasis on collective instead of individual voicing stemmed from years of *lala* movement organizing, whose main concern was to mobilize queer women in forming *xiaozu*, or groups in smaller towns and cities.[68] In this context, the masked feminists are more like "anonymous militants" expressing their anti-sexual-harassment stands, and, at the same, demanding sexual liberty and rights. Besides the prevention of cyberbullying, the masked faces, in contrast with the metal bra and short skirt, further invite the offline and online audience to reflect on the politics of sexual harassment. Masking hence makes a strong statement that simultaneously criticizes sexual harassment and reaffirms sexual autonomy. Moreover, the Shanghai Subway action also illustrates the convergence of *lala* movement and rights feminist movement through the tactics of "masking."

Actively adopting strategies of masking and masquerade, subsequent rights feminists' media knowledge facilitates their agenda setting. During the planning stage of a campaign, one or two spokespersons are chosen to present the whole campaign to the mainstream media. They rehearse what to say to journalists, introduce relevant policy background, and advocate specific policy change.[69] Those who self-identify as YRFAS, for example, are extremely conscious of the potential and limits of mainstream media. Lü Pin, the co-founder of *Feminist Voices* and one of the key organizers of YRFAS, points out that, for an incident to qualify as newsworthy, it has to meet a set of criteria: the protagonist has to come from a group regarded as deserving of attention, instead of a marginalized or stigmatized group; the protagonist should have a clear and focused demand that is not too controversial; and the action and setting of the incident should make a good spectacle.[70] These criteria factor into the campaign planning of YRFAS.

The visual representation of the actions of YRFAS is also carefully thought through. On Valentine's Day 2012, the rights feminists caught public attention with their campaign "Injured Bride," in which three activists wearing bloodstained wedding dresses walked on Beijing's Qianmen Street. The bloodstained wedding dress has been used in multiple anti-domestic violence protests as a dramatic representation of violence in a marriage since 2012. The combination of eye-catching visualizations and placards held by activists that provide a narrative is able to garner significant journalistic interest. Moreover, photos of the act that also capture the placards have a better chance of circumventing Internet censorship. Internet content in China is censored in a number of ways: "the Great Firewall" that blocks foreign websites or services such as Facebook or Twitter; keyword filtering that automatically forbids posts that contain sensitive words or phrases; and real-life inspectors who screen and delete sensitive posts online.[71] These photos with protocol-violating words will have to be deleted by hand and thus have a longer Internet life span. The tactics employed by the feminists to counter online censorship can be seen as acts of masquerading that show their agency in navigating the mediascape.

The advocacy for social change and the intervening practices of YRFAS have forged a new feminist identity and redefined the relationship between feminist activism and the use of media. As elaborated earlier, unlike the feminist pioneers in the 1980s and 1990s who were reluctant to subscribe to the term "feminism" because of its universalizing tendency, YRFAS embraces the notion of rights feminism. At the same time, media activism plays a crucial role in the articulation of rights feminism and the rights feminist identity. The commitment to women's rights is reflected in the Weibo profile description of NMFN, which declares the organization's support for women's human rights. As emphasized by Jun Li, the director of NMFN and a media scholar, striving for women's human rights is a way to resist Chinese liberal intellectuals, who are largely ignorant of gender issues.[72]

In "Social Activism in China: Agency and Possibility," Ching Kwan Lee and You-Tien Hsing identify three types of activism in contemporary China: the politics of redistribution that struggles for material interests such as homeownership, labor rights, and land claims; the politics of recognition that demands moral status, political position, and respect for marginalized identity; and the politics of representation that struggles for expression of ideas in cinema, art, and journalism.[73] While the politics of recognition and representation are influenced by the "flow of universal values, abstract ideas, and virtual images" of "foreign discourses and organizations,"[74] the politics of redistribution tends to be motivated by local injustice. Activism around recognition and representation can forge networks across regions and nations, whereas activism around politics of redistribution is locally bound. They have the ability to forge networks across regions and nations. Although China's current status in international politics and economy means that it cannot be "impervious to international standards of governance and justice,"[75] affiliation with foreign organizations may subject social groups to heightened surveillance and suppression with the introduction of new national security laws under Xi Jinping's rule.

Indeed, the state's control over social activism has tightened since Xi has assumed office as the leader of the state, the Communist Party, and the new government branches charged with internal security. As Yuen points out, cycles of relaxation and repression have characterized the Chinese state's control over civil society since the start of the reform era. However, under Xi, "control . . . has now become the norm and relaxation . . . the exception," and "ad hoc repression of civil society groups and activists is now moving towards a more systematic restriction."[76] The state used to be more lenient towards activism, as long as it had neither foreign funding nor an intent to challenge the rule of the Communist Party,[77] but it has tightened the control in recent years. In particular, activism with nationwide networks and interactions with foreign organizations has faced increasing suppression. The crackdown of feminist activists and their creative responses in the forms of digital masking and masquerade, should be interpreted in this context. In the following sections, I will first focus on masquerading bodies and their digital alterability, and then I will look at collective digital masking and the politics of remaking publicness.

Masquerading Body and Digital Alterability

Existing studies of social media in China (e.g., Weibo or online forum comments) have predominantly focused on discursive formations through text, while overlooking the power of image and bodily involvements. For example, Weibo comments are seen as "hidden transcript," a kind of humorous rearticulation of official discourse to circumvent censorship.[78] The emphasis on textual cues hardly takes into account the effectiveness of visual expressions, such as pictures of protests, handwritten notes, and portraits. The majority of scholarship on Chinese social media tends to equate censorship with state control, and online coded language with resistance. Yang Fan is one of the few who examines the effect censorship has on culture, instead of on state politics.[79] She conceptualizes recoding as a cultural response that articulates the invisible. A "recoding public" comes into being through the making and remaking of meanings. One of her examples is the use of "empty chair" to signify Liu Xiaobo on microblogs. Its significance is beyond circumventing censorship. It's also remaking meanings by toying with the link between language and image.

The digital practices of YRFAS, especially the online display of their bodily performances, can be seen as a negotiation of the relationship between words and images. Staging provocative public performance art or behavior art has been one of YRFAS's most powerful tactics, be it an occupation of a men's bathroom to demand fair bathroom access, or shaving their heads to protest biased university admissions.[80] Visual manifestations could been interpreted as a kind of masking and masquerading. Photographic and videographic documentation of their offline campaigns are uploaded to and widely circulated on Weibo, which would not have been possible on older online platforms such as BBS (Bulletin Board System). Users on Weibo can post screen captures of long text to bypass the 140-word limit or upload derivative works such as Photoshopped pictures that make fun of officials, or counter official narratives.[81]

Masquerading is not always about masking, but also about staging controversial bodily performances for the media. During the 16 Days of Activism against Gender-Based Violence Campaign and the International Day for the Elimination of Violence against Women in November 2012, feminist activists in China launched a petition for the legislation against domestic violence (which was eventually enacted in December 2015.) Although the issue was on the agenda of the National People's Congress, the activists rallied for a more transparent and inclusive legislation process to ensure the content of the law serves victims of domestic violence. The petition also called for more proactive participation from the public, a higher degree of accountability, and expedited passing of the laws.

The activists were hoping to collect 10,000 signatures, but the enthusiastic responses at the outset waned shortly afterwards. Xiao Meili and several members of the YRFAS took self-portraits in a studio and uploaded them via Weibo in hopes of boosting the petition. A cluster of Weibo users who had no personal connections with each other but were following feminist causes joined by posting topless or nude photos of themselves on Weibo with a hyperlink to the petition. A picture uploaded by Xiao Meili to her personal account and the group account of @FeministVoices (Figure 1.2) went viral on Sina Weibo. Inscribed on her torso were two columns of Chinese characters: "Shame on domestic violence / Proud to have flat chest." Notably, three red stripes of text overlay the top, middle, and bottom of the photo, advocating for collecting signatures for legislation against domestic violence. The placement, white italic font and red background of the caption resemble Barbara Kruger's 1989 artwork, which was created to support women's reproductive freedom. By referencing Kruger's work, Xiao highlights the female body as the battleground of the politics of gender, where physical and symbolic violence materialize.

Xiao's photo set the stylistic prototype for some of the subsequent posts.[82] A photo that borrows Xiao's graphic design shows two nude women with what appear as used tampons hanging from their mouths, and what appear as used sanitary napkins adhered to different parts of their bodies. Viewed along with the ten Chinese characters inscribed on their bodies, "menstrual blood is not shameful / domestic violence is reprehensible," these bloodstained sanitary products also resemble

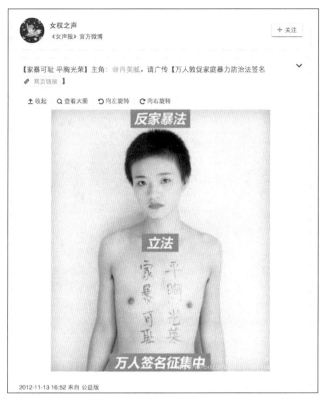

Figure 1.2. Screenshot of Xiao's petition photo soliciting support for legislation against domestic violence publicized through Sina Weibo account @FeministVoices.

bandages covering different injuries from physical assaults. The largest bloodstained cloth covering the women's genital areas can be read as a sanitary napkin or a bandage in this context. The powerful image offers layered interpretations that simultaneously denounce domestic violence and attest to menstruation as an essential female bodily experience that is shamed and hidden from public view. Responding to Xiao's picture, Er Mao's photo adopts Xiao's template, but it differs from Xiao's in important ways. In contrast to Xiao's physical composure and stilted gaze, Er Mao's photo shows her screaming with her eyes closed and hands balled into fists. Instead of inscriptions, her torso is covered with red palm prints that resemble bruises from beatings.

Rather than inviting critical reflection, the unapologetic display of pain from domestic violence stirs a visceral response in the viewer.

The subjects of other photos sought to subvert binary gender norms and aesthetics that prescribe "proper" gender performance: we see masculine women, transgender individuals, and a man wearing lipsticks with the words "I can be sissy, but you can't hit me" inscribed on his body. These pictures repoliticize the body and redefine femininity and masculinity. Despite constant raids on pornographic material online, images that objectify women's bodies are easily available.[83] Female nudes are repurposed by feminists through writing words on bodies and adding text overlays to provoke the public. In her discussion of feminist nudity in Chinese protests, Katrien Jacobs uses "disorderly aesthetics" to describe how nude images are used to "create meaning by soliciting feedback and affective encounters."[84] Here, the use of the body and nudity together with digital alteration of words and images illustrate the practices of digital masquerade.

Collective Masking and Remaking Publicness

As explained in the introductory chapter, the conventional framing of masquerade often deconstructs normative gender identities and challenges heteronormativity, which usually presumes an individualized identity concerning gender and sexuality. My framing of digital masking and masquerade, instead, points to the interface between the medium and the subject, which involves collective efforts in assembling activist activities and remaking publicness. Here I use publicness to describe the state of being public, especially on social media. In the process of assembling, digital masking is an important tactic, especially in the collective bodily appearances of the activists.

One example of collective digital masking is a series of digital photographs by YRFAS released as part of the Free the Five campaign. Most of the creators involved are friends of the Feminist Five. The photographs depict five women, each wearing a mask on which the faces of the Feminist Five are printed, enacting the daily lives of the arrested feminists (Figure 1.3). The five were photographed in mundane settings in Guangzhou carrying out day-to-day activities: eating dim sum, shopping at a wet market, strolling along a river, playing in a public park, and

Figure 1.3. Free the Five group pictures taken on the street of Guangzhou.

resting at the storefront of a sex shop. These pictures, using minimal costs, reassert the relevance of the Feminist Five in quotidian environments. Despite the uncertain treatment of the Feminist Five at the detention center, their fellow feminists use lighthearted and creative collective masking actions to pay respect to their friends and expose the absurdity of the arrest.

Shortly after the online dissemination of these photographs, another group of rights feminists in Beijing created photos of themselves wearing the same masks appearing in different public spaces in their city. It would have been difficult to take these photos on the spot in the heavily guarded capital, so these women digitally superimposed photos of themselves on those of public spaces in the city (Figure 1.4). In this particular example, the feminists used nudity to draw affective responses by digitally putting the bodily displays in front of an iconic architecture, which was the stadium built for the 2008 Beijing Olympics. Like the earlier picture of Xiao Meili, the diversity in terms of heights and shapes of the bodies in this image diverged from the conventionally attractive bodies on commercial media. In both examples, wearing the masks of the Feminist Five declared their relevance in public spaces.

The production mode of these digital photographs is also conditioned by the distribution pattern of social media. As the interactive norm on Weibo encourages daily updates, in the Guangzhou case, for example, dozens of pictures were taken on the same day, while photographs were

Figure 1.4. Free the Five group pictures, with digital alteration, uploaded to the Weibo account @AntiPETD. The words read, "Rights feminism is not guilty!"

released one per day over a period of several days. While the Internet is typically understood as a public space facilitating discussion and community formation, the publicness of the Internet is fraught with exclusions. A study on an environmental NGO's use of the Internet to promote their causes acknowledges that the public sphere online can be elitist, ineffective in reaching out to new supporters, and short of critical exchange.[85] Conceptualizing public spheres as allowing "open debates about issues of common concern, continuous debates and a large number of participants," Adrian Rauchfleisch and Mike Schäfer identify multiple public spheres on Weibo that lie along the continuum between apolitical entertainment and an ideal discursive space.[86] Weibo is a prime example of an Internet platform that could be exclusive and hierarchical. As Marina Svensson points out, there is a participatory gap on the platform, as many registered users are inactive or post infrequently, while a small percentage of users dominate the feed. Sina Weibo's active courtship of celebrities, public intellectuals, journalists, and business leaders privileges their voices over marginalized groups and ordinary citizens.[87] Moreover, social media has been criticized as an individualistic private sphere.[88] The increasing reliance on social media can be construed as an outcome of the failure of representative democracy, a symptom of the failure of "public terrain of political participation."[89] The individualistic, atomized mode of networked participation reflects how the neoliberal logic has eroded "collective public citizenry."[90]

Online media is capable of reinforcing sexism and misogyny in explicit and subtle ways. Wallis shows that ostensibly subversive online derivative works that mock and attack the government are built on visual and linguistic rhetoric that denigrates femininity and reinforce the violation of women's bodies.[91] For example, the Grass-Mud Horse song that went viral on the Chinese Internet plays on the pun between the Chinese name of the animal and the curse "fuck your mother" to criticize the government's censorship of online speech. The rhetoric of criticism embedded in the lyrics is premised on a set of gendered binary relations, in which the trope of the mother represents the sacred motherland penetrated by the evil government. The misogynistic language online sometimes reveals the entangled relations between gender and class in the reform era. One telling example is the term "green tea bitch," which has recently gained currency online. The term was created by Chinese netizens referring to young women of pure, wholesome appearance (suggested by the metaphor "green tea") who offer sexual favors to rich men in exchange for money or material goods. As Cao and colleagues observe, the term implies that women are expected to conform to certain aesthetic standards of femininity in order to be considered "marketable."[92] The YRFAS constantly receives misogynistic attacks online, as evident in the derogatory comments with compound terms such as "feminist bitch" or "feminist cancer" on their postings.

Though the individualistic mode of participation is embedded in the design of Weibo, the tactical use of group accounts by Chinese feminists can be seen as a kind of masking. Here masking is no longer understood in the literal sense of wearing masks but refers to a strategy of collective masking on social media. Besides regular NGO Weibo accounts, many *xiaozu* (small groups) accounts have been established to disseminate alternative and controversial opinions. For example, @InternationalSluts is a group account for sex-positive bisexual and lesbian women. These group accounts rally people across geographical locations and facilitate offline organizing as a way to work against misogynistic attacks online. Besides these feminist articulations from queer women, queer activists also leverage the affordances of the digital platforms to negotiate with censorship. In April 2018, Weibo announced that it would remove content deemed illicit, including posts about homosexuality. A gay Weibo user with many followers tweeted a hashtag that translates into English as "#IAmGay#," which was then retweeted thousands of times and generated a few thousand comments overnight. Many of these retweets used this hashtag to share personal stories of coming out, criticize censorship, and express solidarity. As Sara Liao observes, "isolated personal accounts were connected through Weibo by retweeting, commenting, and liking,"[93] and these accounts contribute to building a counter-discourse that makes queer people visible and challenges the censorship on homosexuality imposed by social media platforms.[94]

YRFAS's strong demand for the accountability of both public and private institutions has accelerated concrete social changes in women's lives. A series of reports and complaints officials have successfully brought the issue of gender discrimination in employment to the court. In August 2012, the media revealed that the admissions system of many higher education institutions set a higher bar of entry for female applicants. After multipronged follow-up actions by rights feminists, the Ministry of Education prohibited higher education institutions from setting gender quota in their enrollment in May 2013. Several years after the online campaign for legislation against domestic violence, China's first anti-domestic violence law took effect in March 2016. The influence of the group accounts such as @FeministVoices and @WomenAwakening demonstrates digital masking and masquerading that point to the interface between the medium and the subjects, which involves collective efforts in assembling activist movements and remaking publicness. This dimension of facilitating collective efforts continues to influence subsequent feminist activism and the collective empowerment of women in the process of fighting against sexual harassment.[95]

Conclusion

The mask of Guy Fawkes, popularized by the main character V in the film *V for Vendetta*, was widely used in the Egyptian revolutions of 2011 and subsequent social protests, including the 2014 Umbrella Movement in Hong Kong. Paolo Gerbaudo argues that the use of masks represents "faith in the democratic power of 'autonomous' individuals and self-organising collectives" in most of the post-1968 alternative social movements.[96] Influenced by notions of "spontaneity and autonomy," masks, tactics of anonymity, and "neo-anarchist" tendencies have been explicit in the self-governance of the Zapatistas in Mexico, the leaderless anti-globalization movement and, more recently, the open-source software movement and hacker collectives such as Anonymous.[97] While the digital masking tactics of YRFAS coincide with global protests in their use of anonymity, digital masking also points to other layers of masking.

As exemplified by the digital masking and masquerading practices of YRFAS, social media such as Weibo gives rise to a new set of feminist aesthetics and politics under state surveillance and censorship. The notion of digital masking and masquerading does not suggest an authentic identity or personhood behind the masks and masquerades, but a process in which the creative usage of social media intersects with the formation of feminist identities and articulations. From the masked actions in Shanghai Subway to the wearing of masks in supporting Feminist Five, their tactics of masking and masquerading are sometimes provocative, seeking affective responses, and other times humorous and lighthearted as they expose the absurdity of state sanctions. Their everyday resistance and negotiations can hardly become large-scale protests in public, which in turn shapes their aesthetics of digital masking and masquerade. As I try to demonstrate in this chapter, this formation of new rights feminism is entangled with *lala* feminism and the queer movement, as illustrated in the masked action of Shanghai Subway.

These practices digital masking and masquerade can be clearly categorized as rights feminism. What kinds of ideas of rights are they referring to? How do activists engage and develop right-related concepts? Recognizing the constitutive role of the media, the following chapter looks at the rich repertoire of new rights feminism, including international human rights concepts, domestic political norms, and rhetoric related to rights, legal activism, and rights-defense.

2

Performative Rights

Practices of Quan

As outlined in the previous chapter, organizations such as Media Monitor for Women Network in Beijing gradually experienced the shift from non-governmental engagement to rights feminist media activism. In 2009, the network started to publish the weekly electronic newspaper *Women's Voice* and launched its website. Browsing through *Women's Voice*, you will find that the term *quan*, or rights, is frequently used in news reports and commentary on issues pertaining to women. Different notions of *quan* appeared in this e-journal, such as *nüquan* (rights feminism), *renquan* (human rights), *quanyi* (rights and interests), and *weiquan* (rights defense), which encapsulate the multiplicity and growth of rights-related discursive and embodied practices. *Women's Voice* alludes to *renquan* (human rights), for example, when making references to international human rights framework, particularly the Convention on the Elimination of All Forms of Discrimination Against Women (CEDAW) and the United Nations World Conferences on Women. The online newspaper also provides information on international women's rights organizations, such as introducing feminist guidelines and the gender monitoring and evaluation methods from the Association for Women's Rights in Development. Notably, the newspaper reports on issues such as the thirtieth anniversary of CEDAW in 2009 and had a special issue on the Beijing 20+ NGO forum in Bangkok in 2014. Beijing 20+ was the twentieth anniversary of the Fourth World Conference on Women held in Beijing in 1995, a milestone for global women's rights.

Apart from drawing upon the notion of human rights and the UN framework, "women's rights and power" (*funü quanli*) refers to women's human rights and fundamental freedoms, including equal rights to education, employment, political participation, access to productive resources, and health and reproductive rights. "Women's rights and interests" (*funü quanyi*) usually refers to women's political, economic, social, educational, and legal rights, which overlap with *funü quanli* in terms of specific content and areas involved. The most common issues include employment discrimination, sexual harassment, sex workers' rights, LGBT rights, domestic violence, gender equality legislation, women's political participation, rural women's rights, maternal and children's rights, and economic statuses. Compared to *quanli*, *quanyi* is more often mentioned in the discussion of legislative issues and references to the Law on the Protection of Women's Rights and Interests. However, in general, *quanyi* often appears in the same article or topic as *quanli* with no clear distinction.

Women's Voice also illustrated a slow emergence of the rights feminist subjectivities by reporting rights feminist activism, including the many cases analyzed in the previous chapter such as the Shanghai Subway action and the anti-sexual harassment photo campaign. In the beginning of the weekly e-newspaper in 2009, the journal emphasized women's development and gender equality. When referring to women and women's rights, the term *funü* was usually used, which can be consistently observed in the official translation of international human rights conventions as well as the domestic legal language. When it was first published in 2009, *Women's Voice* was set to "explore and converge the neglected, overlooked, or isolated information and resources on gender in existing communication system, particularly mass media."[1] On the second anniversary of the weekly e-newspaper in 2011, the editor saw that the e-newspaper had shifted from being an "alternative media based on gendered perspective" to a "rights feminist news criticism weekly."[2] *Women's Voice* thus showed the gradual embrace of and emphasis on identity as rights feminists, as the comments often addressed the readers as rights feminists. The e-newspaper also featured interviews with self-identified rights feminists, including the male intellectual and media critic Chang Ping, who publicly identified as a rights feminist. In 2012, the e-newspaper started to cover the actions of Young Rights Feminist Action School (YRFAS), such as the "Injured Brides," "Occupy the Men's Restroom," and the actions that use naked pictures for anti-domestic violence campaign analyzed in the previous chapter.

Consistent with my observation in chapter 1, the articulations of the rights feminist identities in the e-newspaper *Women's Voice* illustrated the formation of the new subjects of rights. The electronic journal also illustrates the emergence of "rights feminism" in the context of a variety of right-related discourses and practices. What are the historical contexts and technological affordances that contribute to the rise of the myriad of right-related discourse and practices that concern gender and sexuality? How do the different notions of *quan* shift in different contexts, and what is the role of digital media in it? In this chapter, I develop the notion of "performative rights" as a mode of digital masquerade to theorize the processes of rights articulations and the constitutive role of the media. In doing so, I intervene the debates between the "feminist and queer rights liberal paradigm" and the "liberal paradigm critique" outlined in the introductory chapter.

Media and Performative Rights

The scholarly study of the intersection of media and rights is expanding. As suggested by Tumber and Waisbord, there are mainly three branches of the literature. The first one looks at the laws and policies concerning the rights of expression and communication, addressing issues such as state surveillance, censorship, the laws regulating the press, and the limits of the freedom of expression. The second branch delves into the political processes of news making, examining how the state and civil society devise strategies to influence the media to shape the public perception of an issue. The third branch of the literature concerns media representations of human rights, which highlight how some human rights (such as socioeconomic rights and the rights of marginalized populations) tend to be ignored or censored. Moreover, media representation scholars have argued that media, by framing an issue in terms of rights, renders rights as a collective issue requiring shared responsibility and a response from the state. Taken together, the existing research shows that media is both a pivotal institution disseminating the understanding of and debate on human rights, and the very topic of the debates on human rights in issues such as censorship.[3]

Scholars have investigated the relationship between media and rights pertaining to gender and sexuality along the lines of the research identified above. For example, there are journalism studies on how women of different identities and women's rights activism have been represented in media.[4] Moreover, several studies have been devoted to examining how media represents violence against women.[5] Notably, when a news report frames sex trafficking in terms of human rights violations, it is more likely to include survivors' and activists' views.[6] This framing identifies the underlying cause of human trafficking as structural and, thus, calls for a collective action to address the issue. Apart from the media representation of issues related to women's rights, the existing scholarship has also studied the relationship between LGBT rights and media. Some studies have examined how LGBT activists in different places use different digital media platforms to advance their causes,[7] while others have looked at censorship and blocked access to content related to LGBT issues.[8] Transnational LGBT activism taking place online has also been critiqued for its neocolonial discourse that reinforces the perceived backwardness of non-Western societies.[9]

While many of these previous studies conceptualize rights closely resembling the idea of human rights, the multiplicity of *quan* in *Women's Voice* signifies a more complicated meaning of *quan* in the Chinese context. Like *Women's Voice*, contemporary feminist and LGBT rights cover a wide range of rights-related practices, including deploying domestic legal norms, using international rights discourse and legal activism, as well as the rights-defense mode of practices. In this chapter, I develop the notions of performative rights, offering a new perspective to rethink the relationship between media and rights.

In her well-known theorization of gender and performativity, Judith Butler points out that the meanings of gender are not essential or fixed but formed in repetitive acts that are performative.[10] Butler uses the examples of drag, cross-dressing, and the enactment of butch/femme lesbian identities to challenge the presumed view of these practices as "imitation" of the "original" gender.[11] She considers gender as an "act" that is both "intentional and performative."[12] Following Butler's framing of "performative" as "a dramatic and contingent construction of meaning" that can be "effectively disruptive" and "truly troubling,"[13] I consider the discursive and embodied practices of *quan*, or rights by feminist and queer activists as performative acts. I define "performative rights" in three aspects: performative citations of rights, performative tactics of articulating rights, and performative media-centric rights.

First, the performative citations of rights underline the "dramatic" appropriation of the established framework of rights that may be "effectively disruptive" to conventional understandings of rights. Second, performative rights highlight the tactic, flexible, and situational use of rights in different contexts. Third, performative rights accentuate the co-constitutive role of the media. The notion of performative rights as a mode of digital masquerade captures the agency of feminist and LGBT activists in strategically drawing from different notions of *quan*, including the international human rights framework and the domestic legal norms of rights and interests, as well as a media-centric approach to rights defense. Moreover, understanding *quan* as performative sheds new light on the co-constitutive role of media in the formation of discursive and embodied practices.

Drawing from semi-structured interviews with various NGO staff and activists, an analysis of selected NGO documents, and media texts that promote the discourse of *quan*, this chapter analyzes gender/sexuality-related discourse and practices against the backdrop of the globalization of the human rights discourse. I deem *quan* as sites of cultural struggles among stakeholders—including the government, the juridical system, activists, and communities. Specifically, this chapter first historicizes the formation of rights feminism, including the complicated relationship between feminist/queer rights and the human rights framework. Then I look at how activists "perform" in drawing upon different concepts of rights in various contexts. Specifically, I highlight how media is co-constitutive in voicing rights-related concerns, which illustrate the practices of "performative rights." Before I examine contemporary performative rights practices, I take a detour to look at the notion of rights feminism in the Marxist framework in the 1980s, which will illustrate the instability of rights feminism and hence pave the way to understanding its contemporary performative practices.

Historicizing Human Rights and the Resurgence of Rights Feminism

After the founding of the People's Republic of China (PRC) in 1949, the notion of human rights was seen as irrelevant to a socialist country—as the Communist Party had secured Chinese people's rights and, thus, dismissed "human rights" as a bourgeois slogan. Despite how human rights was not able to find a place in revolutionary ideology, demands for human rights were briefly mentioned during the 1957 Hundred Flowers Movement and resurfaced in the late 1970s during the Democracy Wall movement, partly to address the hardship of the Cultural Revolution.[14] Compared to these episodic discussions of human rights in the history of the PRC, rights discourses and rights consciousness have been pro-liferating on a larger scale since the late 1980s. The emergence of rights discourse is related to a series of domestic legal changes, as well as the adoption of a "more positive, active, and participatory approach" of the international human rights framework.[15] China signed the International Covenant on Economic, Social, and Cultural Rights (ICESCR) and the International Covenant on Civil and Political Rights (ICCPR) in 1997 and 1998, respectively.[16]

China's active participation in the international human rights re-gime was usually seen as a post-1989 or post-Cold War effort.[17] How-ever, sorting out the official and intellectual history of women's rights discourse in the 1980s provided a different version of the story. First of all, the Convention on the Elimination of All Forms of Discrimina-tion against Women (CEDAW) was the first human rights treaty China signed and ratified in 1980. China submitted its initial periodic report in 1985 and its second report in 1989. In tracking the international ef-forts of China in adopting the international human rights framework, the 1980s was largely overlooked. Part of the reason, I suspect, lies in the marginalization of women's rights in a broader academic field of human rights research. In the study of the development of gender, most studies have pointed out the crucial role of the 1995 World Conference on Women—with little attention paid to efforts of the understanding of rights, especially women's rights, before 1995.

This book does not detour to trace the understanding of women's rights in the 1980s—when most works were initiated and organized by state-sponsored entity, the All-China Women's Federation (ACWF). Yet a re-reading of a classic feminist piece of writing, Li Xiaojiang's 1983 ar-ticle "Human Progress and Women's Emancipation," can illuminate the complex notion of rights, particularly women's rights at that time.[18] Li's article is a piece of foundational feminist writing in China, which later leads to the establishment of women's studies in China as an academic discipline. It is argued that the historical significance of this article lies in its "essentialist" understanding of women, which challenges the conflation of male-female differences in the socialist era.

As a foundational socialist feminist text (it is grounded in a historical-material developmental understanding of human societies), the essay emphasizes class and its role in configuring the feminist movement while describing the *nüquan* (women's rights) movement as a historical movement dating between the late eighteenth century and mid-twentieth century. Tracing the beginning to concepts of human rights and women's rights derived from the French Revolution, Li sees three class-based streams in the women's rights movement. Li identifies upper-class bourgeois women participating in the fight for political rights, as well as middle-class bourgeois women aiming for a kind of soft feminism that called for practical social benefits. Notably, Li attributes the women's movement that called for political and social rights in early twentieth-century China to the first stream of upper-class activism. Yet Li further argues that the third stream, the liberation of working-class women, was mixed with the proletarian revolution that aimed for human emancipation. For Li, the women's rights movement ended when it was still far from the goal of women's emancipation.

Such a model of understanding the feminist movement addresses neither the fight for women's political rights in a proletarian society nor working-class women in a bourgeois society. The demarcation of class-based womanhood and period-based streams of the women's rights movement does not provide sufficient answers to the questions of the different contexts of the working-class women's movement. Yet the essay should not be dismissed as a failed attempt of mapping out the women's rights movement with the binary categories of a bourgeoisie or proletarian society. Rather, the essay symptomatically reveals the ambivalence toward the notion of women's rights. It demonstrates a strong effort to raise women's issues and the notion of women's rights in an official socialist intellectual framework. As Li states, "the equality between men and women was, in most places in the world, still a measurement of the emancipation of women; yet it is not the ultimate measurement . . . As natural differences exist between two sexes, social differences also exist. . . . Today, women's emancipation is not a stand-alone movement but a stream that converges with the river of human emancipation."[19]

Furthermore, to position the women's rights movement in a state-sponsored Marxist-inspired, if not reductive, narrative of progressive human emancipation, Li's invocation of the women's rights movement provides a peculiar case to raise *nüquan*, or women's rights, prior to the state's gradual embrace of the international human rights framework in the 1990s. In other words, the notion of women's rights has multiple meanings, and its resurgence in post-Mao/postsocialist China is not always tied to the UN human rights framework. This understanding of *nüquan* also differs from the discussion of women's rights in the earlier twentieth century that we explored briefly in the introductory chapter and contexualizes my translation of *nüquan* as rights feminism.

My close reading of Li's article also diverges from the typical view that the term "feminism" was rejected in China in the 1980s, though there were feminist ideas and practices at the time.[20] What Li's article suggests is feminism's relevance within a socialist framework of thoughts. In her article "Towards an Ethics of Transnational Encounters, or 'When' Does a 'Chinese' Woman Become a 'Feminist'?," Shu-mei Shih theorizes precisely this refusal by Li Xiaojiang and other Chinese female intellectuals to be named as "feminist," specifically in a transnational context. Shih analyzes how Li's refusal of Western feminism is related to her suspicion of how American feminists see socialist China as more "advanced" for its earlier state-sponsored equal pay, and some see contemporary China as less "advanced" because of its lack of women's rights. Shih calls this a "value-encoding of time"[21] caused by a kind of Western-centric universalism that constitutes "a self-consolidating epistemology" that in turn sets the standard of subjectivity to be "imitated/affected by the non-Western Other."[22] Notably, disidentifying as a feminist, Li develops a notion of rights feminism in the Marxist framework that illustrates the instability of the term "rights feminism." Recognizing the performative and contextual meanings of rights, the following section looks at how recent feminists and queer activists engage rights performatively on an everyday basis.

"Borrow the Winds": Performative Citations of Human Rights

Like the references to an international women's human rights framework in *Women' Voice*, LGBT activists have taken up the human rights framework in their advocacy work, especially by raising awareness of the issues related to sexual orientation, gender identity, and gender expression (SOGIE). One of the prominent NGOs that engages extensively with the international human rights framework is Common Language. Established in 2005, Common Language is a Beijing-based NGO aiming for public education and the advocacy of sexual and gender diversity. Through community mobilization, public education, and legal advocacy, Common Language is dedicated to raising public awareness of gender and sexual diversity, combating violence and discrimination against LGBT persons, and advocating LGBT equal rights. Common Language has consistently devoted its efforts to making relevant the UN human rights mechanisms, such as using the official rhetoric of China in the UN to influence domestic legal changes.

In 2016, Common Language compiled a document, *LGBTI Rights: From Grassroots to UN*, that clearly explains the relevant UN human rights mechanisms. The document highlights three main UN human rights mechanisms that are important for LGBTI activists: human rights treaty bodies, the Universal Periodic Review, and special procedures.[23] As China has ratified CEDAW, local LGBTI organizations can encourage the CEDAW review committee to ask China SOGIE-related questions, which China must address. The Universal Periodic Review gives opportunities for member countries to provide suggestions to each other. The country under review can either accept or note the suggestion. LGBTI organizations try to ask other countries to give China SOGIE-related suggestions. Latin American countries such as Chile or Argentina are highly desirable candidates for the organizations to approach, as they have better geopolitical relationships with China. The mechanism of special procedures involves UN representatives writing country reports. These representatives include the special rapporteur on the rights to health, the Working Group on Discrimination against Women, and the special rapporteur on extreme poverty and human rights. LGBTI organizations can provide information to these representations.

The priority of this kind of international advocacy is to assist domestic legal advocacy work. The activists use the positive attitudes toward SOGIE in the UN to persuade officials in China or those who are in the law-drafting committee. The activists can use the stand of the government in the UN to convince domestic officials that the government has a positive attitude and commitment toward SOGIE. In China, it is difficult to get a straightforward statement from the government on SOGIE. Sarah, a staff in a LGBTI civil organization, used an "imperial edict" to describe the positive endorsement from the government in this context. She regarded the work of international advocacy as a process to make possible the production of this kind of "imperial edict" and use them to facilitate domestic legislations. In other words, activists "borrow the winds" as a kind of performative citation of, in this case, an international human rights framework. Citing these human rights terms to local state entities, the activists perform rights-related notions that are "disruptive" to mainstream heterosexual culture to make actual social change. In addition to the impact on domestic legislation, the legal advocacy also contributes, however slightly, to the change of China's official rhetoric on the international stage. In a personal interview I conducted with her in 2019, Sarah explained,

> This is a mutual process of influences between the state and the civil society. The government read our report, and they started to use SOGIE terminology to replace terms such as *bianxingren* (transexuals) around 2014. The official rhetoric of China in the UN now usually goes as "We are against all forms of discrimination and violence," including SOGIE. We will imitate this sentence to communicate with domestic officials. We try to speak their language. They also start to speak our language (in the UN context) in order to be politically correct. There is a significant change in adopting SOGIE in the official language, and I think (our organization), as a part of the civil society, plays a crucial role in it.

In other words, NGOs such as Common Language are the co-creators of the meaning of *quan* by using tactics such as "borrowing the winds" to communicate with different levels of government stakeholders. In this process, Common Language "performs" human rights in front of local stakeholders. Here, the development of human rights in China needs some contextualization. Since the "Southern Tour" of Deng Xiaoping in 1991, which set out to deepen the Reform and Open policy, a series of legal changes has taken place.[24] The government passed a series of laws creating important legal rights for citizens and limiting the power of government authorities—including the significant amendment of the

Constitution in both 1999 and 2004, thereby entrenching the rule of law and the protection of human rights. The publication of a white paper on human rights in 1991 led to changes in the Constitution.[25] At the same time, international rights treaties were ratified, and the text of laws now often includes concepts of rights, often in the form of *quanyi*, or rights and interests. When the PRC issued a national human rights action plan in April 2009, it became one of only 26 countries that responded to the UN's call to establish a national human rights plan in 1993. Since 2009, the State Council of the PRC has issued three national human rights plans for the periods 2009–2010, 2012–2015, and 2016–2020.[26] These legal reforms in China represent a transition from rule by law to a Chinese version of the "rule of law."[27] These legal changes manifest what John Erni called "a legal modernity with its own characteristics" which "allows for an increasing rhetorical scope for human rights, resists wholesale legal transplantation seen as foreign intrusion into the state's domestic legal reform process, facilitates the capital process to influence and even govern legal education of judges and lawyers, and proffers new modern Chinese legal subjects that are not only tolerated but actively cultivated."[28]

Following the official rhetoric of "socialism with Chinese characteristics," official discourses on human rights in China constitute a state-endorsed regime "with Chinese characteristics." The official discourse pays more attention to issues such as poverty, access to food and health, and so on. For instance, *Living a Happy Life Is the Primary Human Right*, a white paper on human rights released by China's State Council Information Office in 2019 sees "development" as the primary and basic human right. This state-embraced version of Chinese exceptionalism on human rights supports "a materialist conception of rights improvement—especially in the spheres of food production, housing, health care, sports, and education—and emphasizes these as the material preconditions for a progressive attainment of a fuller range of rights."[29] At the same time, the official discourse on human rights focuses on human rights with Chinese characteristics, which emphasizes collective rights more than individual rights. Along with the release of official government white papers, the official rhetoric on human rights is promoted by The China Society for Human Rights Studies (CSHRS), the largest national academic association on human rights in China, established in 1993. As a member of Non-Governmental Organizations in Consultative Relationship with the United Nations (CoNGO), the, CSHRS publishes an academic journal, *The Journal of Human Rights.* In this context of "human rights with Chinese characteristics," the self-positioning of Common Languages and other NGOs that promote domestic legal change vis-à-vis the UN framework is not static. Notably, the multiplicity of *quan* also expands the scope of gender/sexuality issues from the framework of human rights to sustainable development. As a legal activist explains,

> When we first do international advocacy, we used human rights discourses without much analysis or strategies. We used to operate in [a] very human rights–based framework. Now we are trying to use more development-rights-based framework, which is more acceptable to the Chinese government. . . . Now we are trying to combine SOGIE and Sustainable Developmental Goals (SDG). It is not necessarily a shift in the discourse of advocacy, but a dual track; we still speak human rights in human rights field, but we also want to speak development in the field of development. It all depends on what the government listens [to].[30]

Another example of this "dual track" is to frame employment discrimination based on SOGIE as a violation of rights to employment but, at the same time, a violation of economic empowerment. The special rapporteur on extreme poverty and human rights specifically addressed employment discrimination based on gender identity, which leads to poverty. This dual track framing can be seen as a kind of performative citation that points to the instability of fixed notions of rights and highlights the processes of constructing rights.

This "dual track framing" can be seen as a rise in the adoption of the "rights-based approach," which combines human rights concerns (such as violence against women, an issue shared by both women from the global North and South) and sustainable development, which have gained currency in the global women's movements at the beginning of the twenty-first century.[31] Human rights have become important for development, as they are effective tools to lobby governments and international organizations to provide the conditions for development. Tripp highlights that the global networks are "increasingly initiated and led by women in the South, and even though much of their funding still comes from the North, the perspectives and priorities they offer are their own."[32] Thus, this fact challenges the earlier critique of first-world women dominating the agenda of the global women's movement. This "rights-based approach" that combines women's rights concerns and sustainable development can also be found in feminist and queer activism in China. For example, Oxfam funded the documentary project *The VaChina Monologue*, a thirty-minute film that traces the ten-year history of the localization of Eve Ensler's play *Vagina Monologues*. This project was funded under the scheme of development, in which the fact of poverty was understood in terms of insufficient knowledge of women's bodies and sex. Similarly, the United Nations Development Programme in China has been active in supporting the LGBT community, organizing events, and funding research such as the national report on LGBT issues.[33] Tactics such as "borrow the wind" or "dual-track framing" demonstrate the performative dimensions of rights, especially in activists' performative citations of the international human rights framework, as well as the development framework.

Tactical and Situational Rights: Domestic Legal Norms

In addition to the performative appropriation of the international human rights framework, it is notable that activists traverse between the international framework of *renquan* (human rights) and domestic legal norms of *quanyi*. While the term *quanli* usually serves as a more straightforward translation of "rights," *quanyi* is a disyllablic noun that combines *quanli* (rights) and *liyi* (interests). In the Constitution of the People's Republic of China, rights are often paired with responsibilities when granted to individuals. Notably, the second section of the Constitution is devoted to citizen's rights and responsibilities. However, instead of *quanli*, the term *quanyi*, or rights and interests, is used to describe the protection of ethnic minorities, women, Chinese people overseas, foreigners, and private or nonstate economies and foreign corporations. The term *quanyi* are integral to the official legal discourse. In official discourses, rights and interests are used to translate *quanyi*, such as in the official translation of the Law on the Protection of Rights and Interests of Women. Though I follow this translation, *quanyi*, in my view, can be better translated "rights and benefits," as the notion oftentimes softens the political meanings associated with the notion of rights. The term *quanyi* emphasizes more the economic and social benefits and less the political interests. At the same time, equality between men and women has been an important part of social policy as well as state rhetoric, which is placed under the umbrella of the *quanyi* (rights and interests) of women.

In particular, the Protection of Women's Rights and Interests Law came into force in 1992. The law aims to "protect women's lawful rights and interests, promote the equality between men and women and allow full play to women's role in socialist modernization."[34] The law specifies rights and interests in political rights, culture and education, work, property, personhood, and marriage and families.

Though Article 33 of the Constitution states that the state respects and protects human rights, the notion of human rights appears much less frequently than "rights and interests" in laws and legal documents in general. Hence, the notion of rights and interests serves as a political and legal norm in the domestic legal regime. According to Michele Mannoni, *quanyi* is not the semantic and legal equivalent of "rights and interests." Rather, the phrase retains its etymological meaning of "power" and negatively connotes profit. Moreover, the adjective *hefa* (lawful), which oftentimes describes *quanyi* in legal documents, is used to impose constraints on the rights and interests Chinese people are entitled to, as only lawful rights—and not unlawful ones—are protected.[35]

In contrast to the notion of human rights, *quanyi*, or rights and interests, legitimatizes feminist and queer activism by adapting domestic legal norms. The notion of rights and interests brings new legibility and works well with antistigmatization activities. The term *quanyi* is often invoked in publicity materials and publications or reports of NGOs. For example, the Beijing LGBT Center, established in 2008, envisions a society in which it is possible for "Chinese citizens to enjoy equal rights and interests"[36] in different aspects of life regardless of gender, sexual orientation, and gender expression. One of its antidiscrimination campaigns involves advocating same-sex marriage rights on Valentine's Day. The Beijing Gender Health Education Institute focuses on research, promotion, training, counseling, and community support work in the fields of sexuality, gender, psychological health, and AIDS intervention. It has an advocacy program that promotes gender and sexual equality and diversity. PFLAG China, established in 2008 in Guangzhou, is an NGO that focuses on LGBT parents, friends, and other social networks. Their mission is to create an environment where LGBT people can have the "dignity and equal rights and interests that they deserve."[37]

It is not uncommon to see an organization's mission statement referring to human rights, yet its Chinese version places more emphasis on rights and interests. The different notions of rights are "performative" here, as the same mission statement may convey different notions of *quan* in different languages and to different audiences. The notion of *quan* is "performative" since it is used by activists tactically and situationally. Although many of these organizations make frequent references to human rights conventions or laws, they are careful about directly using the term human rights in framing their works. As Ann, a staff member in a legal advocacy organization, explained in a personal interview from 2019,

> We emphasize SOGIE-related issues in our work, but we do not label ourselves as human rights defenders. . . . When we do international advocacy, others may think you must be China's human rights defender. I have no objection to that; yet we generally position our work as legal advocacy. . . . We show international bodies that our work is solid, and it is based on social movement. When we face domestic parties, we want to show that we are harmless. We don't want to self-censor. Of course, we believe in universal human rights as an organization, but can we put that in our mission statement? I don't think so.

While the concepts of rights provide a framework for several organizations as well as individuals to appropriate domestic legal norms and the international human rights discourse, it is not always the case. On Family Equality, the website of an online petition for legalizing same-sex marriage initiated by a gay couple who sued their local government for refusing to register their marriage in 2015, the initiators explain that their goal is to create legal reforms through which same-sex marriage and heterosexual marriage will enjoy "completely equal rights and interests."[38] Although they use *quanli*, or rights and power, to frame their cause, they also explain on their website that they are reluctant to use the language of *renquan* (human rights). They are wary that using the discourse of human rights to rally support for same-sex marriage risks being trapped in an endless debate on whether marriage is a human right.[39] Instead, by advocating change from the heteronormative terms of the marriage law to gender-neutral terms, the initiators of the online petition regard their goal as the eradication of legally instituted gender norms that regulate the lives of everyone. The activists see that this framing can draw wider support for same-sex marriage. In this case, the activists appeal to domestic political norms and downplay the language of human rights associated with UN conventions and international laws.

The same individual or organization could also invoke various notions of rights. For example, the term *quan* means different things when used by different individual feminists, queer activists, and communal organizations in different contexts. At the same time, the same individual may frame rights differently in different contexts. As Christina, another feminist activist, revealed,

> I tend to say different things to different people. For example, I will not use rights feminism (*nüquan zhuyi*) to describe my line of profession to the mainstream. Instead, I will use "gender equality" or other terms that I think can better facilitate our communication and understanding. When asked about my work, I will say it is, in fact, about gender equality, or it advances women['s affairs] and changes the subordinate position of women, and etc. [*sic*]. So the discourses used are not monolithic, as you sometimes need new discourse to explain your work in certain contexts. . . . I use "rights feminism" with my fellow members in feminist movements or in sharing sessions or discussions when I think there is a need to highlight this perspective. Of course, the term feminism has to be applied in English-speaking contexts; otherwise, non-Chinese speakers may not understand.[40]

The abundant examples show the performative uses of rights for feminist and queer organizations as well as individuals. Christina's shifting use of terms is not unlike Sebastian Veg's observation of how *minjian* intellectuals, or those with grassroots concerns "among the people," have employed a "two-version" strategy: they write uncensored articles online and outside the mainland press while writing self-censored articles for mainland Chinese audiences.[41] Christina's experience also reflects the fact that the identity of "rights feminist" is performative. It is a hat to be worn and taken off. This "performative" dimension of the identity can be further understood in terms of the convergence between rights feminists and queer feminists.

At first glance, the flexible shifting between the international human rights framework and the rights and interests discourse can be well explained by the vernacularization model. The "vernacularization" framework, which has been influential in studying how the international law on violence against women is implemented in different national contexts, aims to show how activists and organizations use different strategies to make human rights relevant and useful to their causes.[42] This model sees the "practices of women's rights" in different national contexts as the intersection of a "global women's rights package" with pre-existing local ideologies, institutions, and social movements.[43] For example, in China, different official and civic organizations serving women perform vernacularizations of the international ideas of women's human rights to different extents.[44] Analyzing the local uses of global women's rights in Peru, China, India, and the United States, Levitt and Merry relate how local organizations work on women's human rights without explicitly describing it as such in everyday interactions.[45] In the process of vernacularization, vernacularizers represent a chain of translators with various degrees of contact with the international community and the local/rural communities. At the same time, the process of vernacularization always interacts with pre-existing political and gender ideologies. For Levitt and Merry, the dilemma of human rights lies in how "rights ideas and practice need to resonate with existing ideologies to be adopted, but to be legitimate as human rights, they have to reflect universal principles."[46]

Following the vernacularization model, Meng Liu, Yanhong Hu, and Minli Liao highlight the translation of women's rights in China as a process of "traveling theory." They compare the translation of women's rights in three types of organizations: government departments, the officially organized NGO (ACWF), and popular NGOs. In government departments, combining international ideas of women's human rights—such as those embodied by CEDAW—with ideologies in China such as collectivism, Chinese state ideologies and interests take precedence over international ideas. "Women's human rights" is seen as a Western individualistic concept and is never invoked, whereas "women's rights and interests" are seen as guaranteed by the Constitution and are promoted.[47] Government-sponsored organizations "strike a compromise between the national legal system of women's rights and interests and the international system of women's human rights" without advocating reform.[48] In contrast, the NGOs play much more active roles. They connect local Chinese women with the international community, with the advocacy of legal reforms to bring Chinese law in accordance with international conventions such as CEDAW. The activists use the term "women's human rights" when they are dealing with international partners, and they talk about "women's rights and interests" when dealing with domestic partners.[49]

The vernacularization framework is crucial in pointing out the relevance of international legal norms and the human rights framework. This aside, the flexible uses of rights discourses can also be seen as "strategic adaptations" to take advantage of the limited opportunities presented to Chinese NGOs,[50] or a strategy of "pragmatic resistance," which is a spectrum of covert-overt actions that innovate strategy and tactics to achieve social change under authoritarian conditions.[51] Moreover, they show how the meaning of rights are not static but performative. In the vernacularization framework, ideas of rights are seen as a one-directional flow that interacts with "pre-existing" ideas. Yet it may overlook the different layers of interactions among different actors, including the government, state entities, activists, and the media. Rather, the notion of "performative rights" captures not only the tactical uses of rights by "borrowing the winds" and the situational uses of rights; it also signifies the co-creation of knowledge and meaning of *quan* by the activists.

Impact Litigation and Media-Centric Rights Defense

Along with the performative practices of using rights in tactical and situational ways, the media also plays a crucial role in the activist actions of "performative rights." The actions that are pursing different notions of rights are oftentimes referred to as rights defense (*weiquan*) and are usually "court-centric." The term "rights defense" gradually changed from a discourse that focused on state-socialist duties in the early 1990s to a discourse that focused on legality and rights in the 2000s.[52] The emergence of *weiquan* lawyers, or what Fu Hualing and Richard Cullen call "rights protection" lawyers, is caused by the privatization of the legal process in China, in which lawyers used to be civil servants. A key feature of the lawyering, according to Fu and Cullen, lies in the acceptance of the legitimacy of the existing political system, constitutional constraints, and legal framework.[53] It is, by and large, a court-centric system to resolve conflict in order to maximize the rights and interests of a client. While more recent studies on rights defense predominantly focus on struggles for labor rights, property rights, and land rights, feminist and queer activism points to a more diverse understanding of *quan*.

A series of legal services to women were made available throughout the 1990s, including the establishment of the first women's hotline in 1992, the Women's Legal Research and Service Center in 1996, and Beijing Maple Women's Consulting Service Center in 1996.[54] While many of these services had institutional support from universities and other research facilities, they gradually changed to nonofficial organizations. Male homosexuality used to be punished using "hooliganism" from Article 160 of the Criminal Law. In 1997, "hooliganism" was removed; hence, there was no more legal basis for prosecution of male homosexual activities. In 2001, the Chinese Psychiatry Association removed homosexuality from its medical category of perverts. Generally, these changes are seen as the decriminalization and depathologization of homosexuality in China, and they brought about more visibility of and positive discussions on homosexuality. However, other forms of legal, medical, social, and cultural oppression of homosexuals and other sexual minorities remain. More recently, LGBT legal services and associations were created, such as the establishment of the Rainbow Law Hotline. Established in 2015, the hotline service features legal scholars and practitioners who provide legal advice on issues faced by LGBT people, as well as the claim of custodial rights by LGBT individuals. The latter case involves parents in "nominal marriages," where one or both partners are LGBT individuals. The hotline also offers services to those whose "rights and interests are seriously violated," such as being forced by parents to get married or being offered conversion therapies by doctors.

The earlier legal services are "court-centric," while the latter practices are more "media-centric." Besides providing legal services, feminist and queer organizations used the language of rights defense to frame their cultural events in advancing women's social status and well-being in the 2010s. For example, one of the aims of the China Women's Film Festival, which started in 2012, is to address the "issues of rights defense faced by women in China and abroad."[55] The festival showcases films produced by women, films with female leads, and stories with women's experience as their thematic concern. While not every film is directly linked to rights defense, a notably case is that filmmaker Fan Popo successfully sued the State Administration of Press, Publication, Radio, Film, and Television after his documentary *Mama Rainbow* was removed from major video-hosting websites in China. Featured in the documentary *Block and Censor*, Fan described his action as "picking up the weapon of law to defend my own rights and interests."

While rights-defense actions are often seen as "court-centric" practices that rely on lawyers, the activists also appropriate the term "impact litigation" to frame their actions. Impact litigation is a conscious strategy of using litigation cases to influence public policy and seek social change. Using the rights-defense approach, the activists request for information disclosure from government bodies such as the Ministry of Education and the State Administration of Press, Publication, Radio, Film, and Television[56] by using the Regulation on the Disclosure of Government Information. They also use the rights of employment to frame their cases against the employers who fire them after learning about the employee's HIV-positive health condition or their sexual orientations. In addition, activists use the rights of personal liberty to sue hospitals and clinics that provide reverse therapies to treat gay men.

In the process of making rights claims in media-based rights activism, new claimants such as rights feminists and LGBT people have become visible. Activists constantly use rights-related concepts to frame their actions, especially in litigation cases. Rights are used to refer to a variety of issues—such as education, employment, access to information, and so on. In May 2015, Qiubai made a request to the Ministry of Education for disclosing how they screen and approve textbooks used at universities. She framed her case as lesbians' "right to reputation" (*mingyu quan*) and "right to receive an [*sic*] accurate knowledge in education" (*shou jiaoyu quan*). In this process, the plaintiff's sexual orientation or gender identity was emphasized. The identity of sexual minorities is crucial in framing the rights claim.

Moreover, in the context of media-based activism, "impact litigation" means the impact on increasing public awareness via domestic and international reportage of the court cases. Young, one of the plaintiffs, remarked that the final ruling of the lawsuit was not that important, and he was not planning to win the case. Rather, it was more important to raise awareness about this issue among people who were not gays or lesbians, and to encourage other gays and lesbians to fight for their rights through disseminating the information of the case in the media.[57] Here, media advocacy is not only the means but also the ends of this kind of activism. Performative rights also point to the role of the media in impact litigation and rights defense. In this process, identities such as rights feminist, lesbian, transgender, and gay men were highlighted as rights claimants.

In the practices of "media-centric" rights defense, the notion of "performative rights" captures multiple uses of technology in media-based *quan*-related articulations—including media activism with explicit legal demands and legal services with social media components. The media is often understood as facilitating or limiting feminist and queer social movements, including the articulation of feminist and queer rights. However, the notion of performative rights highlights not only how activists use different media forms to disseminate rights ideas or how the media pluralizes the articulations of human rights but also how the media and rights articulations are mutually constitutive.

Conclusion

This chapter has generated a rich set of empirical data on how feminist and queer activists mobilize various rights discourses through the media and cultural practices. Activists use digital media to engage, develop, or challenge rights-based concepts related to gender/sexuality. At the same time, different media platforms and institutions shape gender/sexuality rights advocacy. The idea of *quan*, embodied in various versions of new rights feminism and LGBT rights, was practiced in tactical, flexible, and situational uses of rights, including international human rights, domestic political norms, and rights defense. These processes of performative citations of rights, performative tactics of articulating rights, and media-centric rights constitute what I call "performative rights."

My focus on *quan* questions the Eurocentrism embedded in the human rights discourse. At the same time, the usages of *quan* in feminist and queer media differ from the officially endorsed regime of "human rights with Chinese characteristics." The official discourse on human rights, exemplified by the publications affiliated with CSHRS, emphasizes human rights with Chinese characteristics. I see *quan* as a type of cultural specificity that differs from cultural authenticity. In this way, this chapter has offered new conceptualizations of *quan* as the mediation of feminist and queer rights that problematizes the Eurocentric, normativized, and teleological conceptions of rights without falling into the trap of Chinese cultural exceptionalism. In this way, my idea of performative rights expands on the "feminist and queer rights liberal paradigm" that stresses the usefulness and importance of the rights discourse yet at the same time cautions against the unintended consequences of mobilizing the discourse of rights raised by the "liberal paradigm critique." Paradoxically, critique of the liberal rights paradigm may perpetrate the understanding of rights as imperialist and exploitative, and overlook the complexity and plurality of the *quan*, or rights, that I have outlined.

I also use performative rights to highlight how media and the processes of human rights practices constitute each other. This shows that digital media is much more than the means for disseminating human rights ideas. Instead, digital media and rights articulations are mutually constitutive. The notion of performative rights draws a theoretical link between rights and digital media in the form of overlapping social processes and formations. As such, performative rights offer an expanded notion of rights that considers not only the bearer of rights but also the process of rights articulation. In the following chapters, I shift from the discursive and historicized analysis of new rights feminism and queer activism to the study of specific digital forms of queer cultures. In order to investigate the co-constitutive relationship between various feminist and queer articulations and different digital media forms, I identify digital filmmaking as a primary site of feminist and queer articulations. The following three chapters will look at community digital filmmaking, exhibition, as well as dating app platforms, respectively.

3

Queer Becoming

Community-Based Digital Filmmaking

In the previous two chapters, I look at how feminist and queer NGOs play important roles in the rise of the new rights feminism, queer activism, as well as the practices of *quan*. Among them, several LGBT NGOs stand out, including Common Language, Beijing LGBT Center, PFLAG China, Beijing Gender Health Education Institute (BGHEI), and Chinese Lala Alliance, which were all established in the 2000s. What are the specific practices that these NGOs use in their promotion and advocacy of sexual diversity, including the ideas of rights? One of the widely used forms is community-based digital filmmaking. For example, the Queer University (*kuer daxue*) program that started in 2012 is a yearly, weeklong documentary workshop organized by the Beijing Gender Health Education Institute (BGHEI). Chinese Lala Alliance, a transnational advocacy group for Chinese lesbians and trans women mentioned in the previous chapter, organizes the China Queer Digital Storytelling Workshop, which seeks to empower Chinese LGBT communities through self-expression and video production. As indicated by the Chinese name of the workshop, the Journey of Self-Discovery, the workshop facilitates the creation and articulation of selfhood through the creation of video shorts.[1] Similarly, Common Language, another NGO that focuses on queer women, has hosted a series of video workshops called We Want to Speak Out, which aims at promoting gender diversity and equality.

In this chapter, I identify digital filmmaking as an important arena for queer articulations. Specifically, I focus on the queer documentary *Comrade Yue*, one of the films that was made in the community-based workshops. Against the backdrop of neoliberalized governance of selfhood, this new wave of community-based queer documentaries, exemplified by *Comrade Yue* (directed by Jianbo Yue, 2013), embodies what I call the "aesthetics of queer becoming" as a mode of digital masquerade in three ways. First, video-making has become an act of coming out through testimonial, confessional, or performative modes of sound-image relationships, especially with the creative use of singing and voice-over with accents. Video is a vital medium to work *through and within* the processes of identification and community formation. In particular, I borrow Hamid Naficy's concept of "accented cinema" and recent queer Sinophone scholarship to look at accented voices in the video. Second, the expressive personal histories in these videos contest the "authentic" homosexual subjects that function as objects of knowledge in mainstream media. The bodily corporality on screen and the intimacy of the video apparatus operate as an interrogation of identity that intervenes in the ongoing discursive debate between the biological determinist and social-constructionist views on homosexuality within the LGBT community in China. Third, the social self constructed in the video intersects with other social issues, which renders queer becoming as an ongoing project of undoing heteronormativity and homonormativity. As I argue, the medium of the video, with its capacity for dissemination online, functions as a unique format that gives rise to a new set of queer aesthetics and politics through first-person audiovisual constructions.

The Proliferation of Sexualized Digital Selfhood in Neoliberalized China

The digital video (DV) camera was introduced into China in the late 1990s, lowering the barrier to documentary and independent video production in terms of cost and equipment. The availability of personal computers also made the editing of these digital videos accessible. Digital technology has facilitated the emergence of a new wave of audiovisual production online that is not related to film studios or TV productions resources. The proliferation of these videos is described as China's new "cinema of dispersion" that is marked by "digital technology, network-based media and portable media player platforms."[2] Many have theorized that this "new Chinese digital cinema" and its aesthetics expanded on the New Documentary Movement that emerged in the late 1980s. The New Documentary Movement, a term coined by Xinyu Lü, began "with rebellions both inside and outside the dominant media system,"[3] especially in opposition to the conventions of the "special topic program" (*zhuantipian*), the model of Chinese television report-age.[4] This "new Chinese digital cinema" reflects the notion of *xianchang*, being "here" and "now," which crystalizes the urgency of these films in relation to social change and everyday life, and their capacity to bear witness to history.[5] Paola Voci used "lightness" to highlight the act of individual production and viewing of "smaller-screen" films in her book *China on Video*.[6] Others find that this new wave of digitalized cultural production "treasures immediacy, spontaneity, and contact with lived experience over the high levels of manipulability associated with the special effects culture of mainstream cinema."[7]

In particular, scholars have pointed out the centrality of individual-ity in these audiovisual works. For example, "iGeneration" is used to describe a new generation of (moving) image-makers in which the "i" indicates "an increasing concern with individual self-expression and self-realization, 'relying on oneself' in uncertain times, and the preva-lence of an increasingly solipsistic directorial style among independent film practitioners,"[8] which aligns with what Yunxiang Yan has called "the individualization of Chinese society."[9] At the same time, the "i" signi-fies information technology in which the Internet, and personal media technologies have facilitated a "post-cinematic culture of amateur pro-duction and transformed cinema" for online viewing.[10] Similarly, Qi Wang observes the rise of "personal filmmaking" across feature film and experimental videos, specifically in the independent filmmaking sector. Wang identifies "a similar keen interest in the trope of personal memory, the intricate relation between past and present, and the inscription of the self in the representational text."[11]

The proliferations of audiovisual constructions of the self coincide with the increasing use of neoliberal technologies of governance. The relationship between neoliberalism and China is complicated. Though Chinese government never uses neoliberalism in describing the current state of China, neoliberal discourses and values have emerged in people's daily lives. Many scholars, especially anthropologists, have observed dominant and prevailing neoliberal trends in contemporary China, such as "neoliberal re-structuring," or neoliberalism as a national project to imagine global reordering.[12] David Harvey contends that contempo-rary China is experiencing neoliberalization with "Chinese characteris-tics" through "accumulation by dispossession," or a neoliberal shift that dispossesses the public of their money or land, centralizes wealth and power in the hands of a few, and thus restores class differences.[13]

In neoliberalized China, with the decrease of social welfare and the increase of privatization, mass media such as television and film is replacing the state in shaping the audience's daily life, especially in cultivating a sense of self and the governance of the self. Although the gender politics on mass media, especially television, are contradictory, it is important to recognize the structuring power of mainstream media in cultivating the sense of neoliberalized selfhood that is aligned to the agenda of the state. This is salient when discussing the negotiating potential of independently produced videos or other UGC (User Generated Content) online.

As Alexandra Juhasz points out, YouTube's design and ownership rely upon "popularity, humor, speed, shallowness, celebrity, and distraction," weakening "the depth of dialogue, the ability to find and link data, the ability to sustain intimate and committed community, and structures of order and discipline" that are crucial to scholarly inquiry.[14] Similar to YouTube, popular Chinese online video websites such as Youku and Tudou in China tend to be dominated by domestic as well as foreign TV drama and reality shows, while the user-uploaded items remain a limited portion of the mediascape. For example, the discourse of neoliberalism has been reflected in matchmaking TV shows such as *If You Are the One* via "market rationality in the dating market, the gendered restoration of class, and the techniques to improve the self."[15] Here, female participants are constantly evaluated and expected to transform into a "proper" candidate for the dating market under "professional" guidance. Television, together with other advice literature, continues to shape the sense of selfhood in terms of health, body, and gender as well as sexuality.

In the context of neoliberalized governance of predominantly heterosexual selfhood on mainstream media, I turn to a specific online video, *Comrade Yue*. The digital video *Comrade Yue* is among a new wave of community-based, queer-themed documentaries primarily organized by NGOs that promotes sexual and gender diversity. These digital videos were usually made in the participatory workshops held in various cities across the country. These workshops provided a platform for participants to master video production skills and discuss gender diversity and equality advocacy. The community-based video workshops were often conducted in affordable hotels or workspaces where tutors and students gathered for intense training. These workshops are also geographically diverse. Besides major cities such as Beijing, Shanghai, and Guangzhou, a handful of workshops have also taken place in cities such as Hangzhou, Wuhan, and Xi'an. Specifically, the director of *Comrade Yue*, Jianbo Yue, participated in the weeklong documentary workshop of the Queer University program organized by BGHEI. After completing the workshop, Yue's proposed project on filming himself was selected and funded, and he made this thirty-minute documentary. This video was released online through Queer Comrades, a long-running LGBT video webcast in China also sponsored by BGHEI.

Many of the videos produced in these community-based workshops are articulations and reinventions of multiple selves enacted through the construction of image and sound. These videos are mainly distributed online through major video websites while also playing an important role in organizing events such as queer film festivals within the LGBT community. The proliferation of these videos—online and offline—coincides with increasing attention to selfhood and the emergence of neoliberal technologies of governance. With the decline of social welfare and the increase in privatization in contemporary China, mass media such as the Internet and television are replacing the state in governing the audience's daily life, especially in cultivating a sense of the gendered and sexualized self. In the rest of the chapter, I will examine how *Comrade Yue* embodies the aesthetics of queer becoming that negotiate the neoliberalized regulation of sexualized selfhood.

Comrade Yue: Audiovisual Articulations of Identity and Selfhood

Comrade Yue (2012) is an autobiographical documentary chronicling the life of the filmmaker Jiaobo Yue, a rural miner who accepted his homosexuality and divorced his wife after a six-year marriage (Figure 3.1). Comrade, or *tongzhi*, is a term that used to describe revolutionary brotherhood and sisterhood, which has been actively used by the Chinese LGBT community to represent sexual minorities. The protagonist

Figure 3.1. The poster for *Comrade Yue* (directed by Jianbo Yue, 2012). Image courtesy of Beijing Gender Health Education Institute.

of this documentary lives in a small town in Shanxi Province, representing the largely overlooked group of gay men in rural China.

In a departure from the conventional approach of representing LGBT people as authentic subjects, this documentary is an "essay film," which Paul Arthur sees as "a meeting ground for documentary, avant-garde, and art film impulses."[16] This film is episodic in nature and filled with performative elements and lyrical expression. The film is structured into several black-and-white singing sequences. All of the film's songs were written and performed by Yue except for the closing song, "All Punks Are Sissies," which is by a Shanghai punk band called Top Floor Circus. The sequences feature facial close-ups of Yue (Figure 3.2) performing the songs he himself wrote and at times looking directly into the camera.

Besides the physical appearance of Yue's body on screen, the presence of his sense of selfhood is salient through the use of sound, particularly through the singing sequences and his accented voice-over. In between these singing sequences are images of different aspects of Yue's everyday

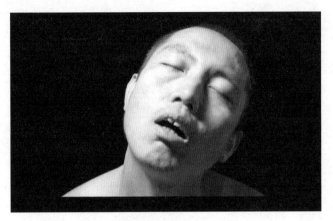

Figure 3.2. Yue sings to the camera in *Comrade Yue*. Image
courtesy of Beijing Gender Health Education Institute.

life, accompanied by his monologues in Mandarin with an accent of
Shanxi dialect that create a loose narrative of his life. The narrative and
the singing sequences in dialect create an interesting tension. The opening of the film consists of a series of shots in his apartment, such as a
close-up of his divorce papers, wedding picture, luggage, his wife eating
noodles, etc. This is the moment when Yue's wife is leaving their apartment after signing the divorce papers. The sequence that follows is of
Yue repeatedly singing, "I want to cry." Here image and sound have a
complicated relationship, as the lyrics sometimes add new meaning to
the previous sequence of images. The singing sequence here adds a sub-
jective and emotional interpretation to the images.

This relationship between sound and image is also layered through
the tension between the image and the emotionally charged voice-over.
The scene chronicling Yue's return to his rural Shanxi hometown where
he honors his ancestors includes mundane shots of him moving bags
filled with coal. The voice-over tells of Yue's complicated relationship
with his father and how as a child he felt ashamed of his father's occupation when he and his companions saw him covered with coal dust.
The image and voice-over create tension, as Yue strongly desires to work
in the coal business, yet the image shows him physically entrapped by
heavy and repetitive labor, a commentary on the lack of social mobility

in contemporary China. Here, the video is, as Michael Renov points out about the documentary form, "a facilitator to self-examination."[17]

The first-person audiovisual constructions about queer subjectivities in everyday context are significant in two ways. First, the use of accented monologues and singing, and the complex image-voice relationship, create a textual heteroglossia that deserves more unpacking. In his conception of the accented cinema, Hamid Naficy proposes a spectrum of exilic, diasporic, and postcolonial filmmakers who explore their ethnicities and identities according to their relationships between home and host cultures.[18] Although Naficy's concept is developed in a transnational context, *Comrade Yue* can be seen as an example of what he calls an "accented video," pointing to the "unhomeliness" a queer individual often experiences in the environment they live in. Here, the accented voice can be further illuminated by recent queer Sinophone scholarship and its awareness of the politics around language, dialect, and accent. Inspired by Shu-mei Shih's concept of "Sinophonic articulations" that are "outside China and on the margins of China and Chineseness,"[19] the emerging field of queer Sinophone studies is more inclusive of queer Sinophone cultures and incorporates the Chinese diaspora in Southeast Asia, Hong Kong, Taiwan, and other places. Queer Sinophone studies, as Howard Chiang points out, "crystallizes Chineseness and queerness as cultural constructions that are more mutually generative than different, as open processes that are more historically co-produced than additive."[20] The notions of the Sinophone and the queer have a "structural affinity"[21] in that both "resist the doxa and hegemony of binary thinking, essentialism, and disciplinarity."[22]

While most of the case studies in queer Sinophone scholarship look at articulations outside mainland China as part of the call to decenter China, considering examples within China can further illuminate the heterogeneity of "Chineseness." For example, veteran queer filmmaker Cui Zi'en from China has continued to make a series of fictional films such as *Men and Women* (1999), *Enter the Clowns* (2002), *Feeding Boys, Ayaya* (2003), and *My Fair Son* (2005). Audrey Yue sees Cui's films, among other works that utilize digital video (DV) technology, as exemplifying queer Sinophone cinema within China, which "questions the ontology of kinship and the new neo-liberal queer subjectivities that are produced by the global reordering of Chinese modernity."[23] In the case of *Comrade Yue*, Yue's accented voice, like his homosexuality, holds a marginal place in society. His homosexuality is expressed in and through the multiple forms of his accented voice such as monologue, singing, and short dialogue with others. In turn, his accented voice also marks his departure from a middle-class, cosmopolitan culture of gay men. Here, Yue's subaltern Chineseness and queerness are, in Chiang's words, "mutually generative" and "co-produced," hence serving as a clear example of queer Sinophone articulation.

Apart from the significance of the accent in the video, the expressive personal histories articulated in the video are also significant because *Comrade Yue*'s articulation of queer subjectivity cannot be simply subsumed under the discourse of coming out. In the scene where Yue is talking about his hobby of marathon running, the voice-over transforms the meaning of the images. It is not until the middle of the marathon scene, when Yue talks about his fantasy of men helping him reach the end of the marathon, that the audience gets the clear message that Yue is sexually attracted to men. In the singing sequence that follows, Yue moans loudly, and this leads to a scene where the camera films him and his lover lying in bed and chatting. Then the camera records Yue having sex with another man. A filter is added to create a shaking and blurring effect so the video can be uploaded for online viewing and entered in documentary competitions such as the Phoenix Documentary Awards organized by Phoenix Satellite Television. This scene demonstrates a mediated intimacy in which Yue self-consciously uses the camera to manifest his sexuality on screen, which is a queer tactic to move beyond identitarian categories by de-emphasizing the identity of gay men and presenting a complex yet poetic representation of his life.

In *Desiring China: Experiments in Neoliberalism, Sexuality, and Public Culture*, Lisa Rofel argues that neoliberalism gives rises to new subjectivities centered around desire, including gay identities.[24] The emergence of these new subjectivities gives rise to a new set of identity politics in contemporary China concerning the circulation of terms such as *kuer* and LGBT by sexuality-related NGOs since the 2000s. In particular, there are conflicting views of "naturally born" homosexuality verses "socially constructed" homosexuality. Organizations such as Aibai.com and PFLAG China (Parents, Friends, and Family of Lesbians and Gays China) proclaim that sexual orientation is "naturally born," "unalterable," and "similar to one's race or skin color."[25] As a reaction against conversion therapy that forces homosexuals to "return to normal," they advocate the view that homosexuals are naturally born and thus unchangeable. In contrast, the Chinese Lala Alliance uses *kuer*, or queer, to signify gender/sexual fluidity, boundary crossing, and the challenging of gender/sexual categories, in opposition to the "homosexuals are naturally born" discourse. Against the backdrop of this ongoing debate between the biological determinist and social constructionist views on homosexuality within the LGBT community in China, the bodily corporality on screen and the intimacy of the video apparatus in *Comrade Yue* operate as a multi-dimensional articulation of identity through sexual fantasy narrative and corporal sex acts, rather than a simple discursive confirmation. Here, *Comrade Yue* illustrates the logic of digital masquerade, where queer expressions, accented voice, and the technological form of digital video are entangled.

Personal as Communal: Community-Building through Video-Making and Circulation

Comrade Yue can be seen as an expansion on a new wave of queer-themed documentary that is influenced by the organization of communities; this new wave requires contextualization here. Homosexuality has been heavily censored in mainstream media. It was explicitly prohibited in film, and publications containing homosexual content are also regarded as pornographic and obscene by the authorities. Film Censorship Regulations issued by the Ministry of Radio, Film, and Television in 1997 prescribe that plots, language, or images specifically portraying sexual promiscuity, rape, prostitution, or homosexuality should be deleted or modified. The General Administration of Press and Publication (GAPP) issued the *Provisional Regulations Concerning Appraising Obscene and Sexual Publications* in 1988, which instructs the press and publication sector to identify pornographic and obscene publications. According to the *Provisional Regulations*, such publications include "salaciously and concretely describing homosexual acts or other perverted acts, or concretely describing violence, abuse, or humiliating acts related to perversion."[26] In recent years, however, as the HIV virus is increasingly treated as a major social health issue by the state, more and more news programs interview people who are HIV-positive, including a number of gay men. These homosexual men are usually seen as the "authentic" homosexual subjects that function as objects of knowledge in mainstream media. In the art-house feature film realm, films such as Chen Kaige's *Farewell My Concubine* (1993)[27] and Zhang Yuan's *East Palace West Palace* (1996) stimulated public attention and scholarly discussion about homosexuality. In *Celluloid Comrades*, one of the earlier monographs that look at homosexuality in Chinese cinemas, Song Hwee Lim examines how the effeminate gay men stereotyped in these two films reconfigure power relations through the "dynamics of resistance-via-obedience."[28] Though these films featured male same-sex desires and received critical attentions at home and abroad, few of these more established films deal directly with the reality and everyday lives of homosexuals in contemporary times. At the same time, other scholarship focuses on fandom and the consumption of popular culture intersecting with gender and sexuality in popular media phenomena, such as the Super Girl singing contest.[29] Although much fan literature such as BL (boy love) stories or drawings increasingly use homosexual acts as narrative tropes, they carve out a fantasy space that remains distant from the reality of the everyday struggles of LGBT-identified individuals.

By way of contrast, in the independent sector, a body of documentaries about sexual minorities began to emerge around the turn of the millennium. Zhang Yuan's *Miss Jing Xing* (2000), Chen Miao's *The Snake Boy* (2002), Zhang Hanzi's *Tangtang* (2004), and Jiang Zhi's *Xiang Pingli* (2005) focus on transsexuals or cross-dressers. Ying Weiwei's *The Box* (2001) is considered to be the first documentary about lesbians in China. These documentaries made by filmmakers who may not consider themselves as LGBT individuals often portray their subjects as isolated individuals. As queer activism continues to expand, independent documentaries record as well as facilitate community organization. Later works such as Shi Tou and Ming Ming's *Dyke March* (2004) and *Women Fifty Minutes* (2006), Cui Zi'en's *Queer China, Comrade China* (2008), and Fan Popo's *Chinese Closet* (2009), *Mama Rainbow* (2012), and *Papa*

Rainbow (2016) have much stronger expressions of LGBT subjectivities and emphasize communal efforts to promote sexual and gender diversity. As Luke Robinson has pointed out, the digital videos made by queer filmmakers such as Cui Zi'en and Fan Popo circa 2010 represent the queer body in a way that asserts queer desire and identities, and thus challenge the conventional voyeuristic objectification of the queer body in documentaries made by heterosexual directors.[30] Comparing the two early documentaries on lesbians, *The Box* and *Dyke March*, Shiyan Chao points out that *The Box* sits uneasily with some aspects of LGBTQ politics, while *Dyke March* shows the filmmakers' sensitivity, sense of responsibility, and political activist agenda, in relation to their subjects.[31]

Notably, these digital videos demonstrate a clear "communal turn" in their themes as well as modes of production. *Queer China, Comrade China* chronicles the history of queer activism and records the history of the community in China. In *Mama Rainbow*, a documentary short about queer individuals and their mothers shot in 2012, there is not much interaction among the six mothers interviewed. In the subsequent 2016 film *Papa Rainbow*, with the support from PFLAG China, the fathers perform as actors in an interactive theater and play out real-life scenarios, including coming out, on the stage. They discuss the plays with other community members, such as other LGBT parents and children. The two documentaries, made four years apart, indicate the more frequent activity within the organization of the queer community. More recently, *Shanghai Queer* (2019), directed by Chen Xiangqi, revisits multiple sites in the city and reconstructs the history of queer activism with a strong urge to record community history. Many of these filmmakers are involved in community work, and Bao has used "queer generation"[32] to describe the cluster of filmmakers associated with Beijing Queer Film Festival, who also played important roles behind the Queer University. Besides the communal turn, this diverse body of digital video documentaries continue to expand in thematic as well as aesthetic forms. Dajing's short video *I Am Going to Make Lesbian Porn* (2014), for example, plays with the audience's expectations by showing the difficulties in making a lesbian porn film for the female audience using the docudrama format.

Comrade Yue is one of the videos in this new wave of queer-themed documentary that is marked by both the communal turn of organizing as well as experimental aesthetics. Specifically, the making and circulation of *Comrade Yue* are sponsored by the community-based documentary workshop Queer University and the webcast Queer Comrade, both under the NGO Beijing Gender Health Education Institute (BGHEI). Wei Xiaogang, Fan Popo, and Yuan Yuan are the three major actors in the Queer University project. Queer Comrades serves as an important distribution venue to raise awareness of LGBT issues and foster a sense of community.[33] Wei Xiaogang is the director of the BGHEI, which hosts a series of media-related projects such as China Rainbow Media Awards (2011–), *Queer Comrades* Video Webcast (2007–), and Queer University documentary workshop (2012–). Both graduates of the Beijing Film Academy, Fan Popo and Yuan Yuan are filmmakers with extensive practical experience and active community engagement. Fan Popo has made several documentaries on themes such as transgender sex workers, parents of gay and lesbian individuals, and *Vagina Monologues* performances in China. Fan's films are shown at international LGBT film festivals. He has been actively involved in the Beijing LGBT Center, Beijing Queer Film Festival, and similar venues. Yuan Yuan has been working closely with the veteran queer filmmaker He Xiaopei and the Pink Space Sexuality Research Centre in using images to explore non-normative sexualities. They use digital filmmaking to conduct participatory projects with those who are usually marginalized in sexuality or HIV/AIDS-related issues, such as women, children, and people with disability.[34] In collaboration with He Xiaopei, her recent work, *Our Marriages: When Lesbians Marry Gay Men*, documents four marriages between lesbians and gays who face tremendous social pressure to get married. Like other LGBT NGOs, BGHEI secures funding primarily from international foundations or organization such as the Ford Foundation, European Union, Oxfam, or Amnesty International.

Queer University recruits eight to twelve students each year. The students pair up and collaborate to make a short film by the end of the class. Many of them come to the training camp with a proposal in mind. More than forty people have participated in the program, and around twenty short films have been made over the last three years at Queer University. These works are available online on the Queer Comrades video webcast as well as major video websites. The digital videos have also been circulated in a network of queer subcultures highlighted by Beijing Queer Film Festival or China Queer Independent Films screenings.

Participating in the Queer University workshop has been a transformative experience for Yue. He divorced his wife one week after finishing the workshop and started to film every aspect of his own life and come out to many of his friends and family. With the help of QU instructor Yuan Yuan, Yue managed to select from his abundant footage and edit it into its current form. For Yue, video becomes a medium through which he identifies and articulates his identity. After its completion, the full-length documentary *Comrade Yue* was released online on the website of Queer Comrades.[35] Launched in 2007, the Queer Comrades website is a long-term platform for LGBT videos, and it also uploads videos on major Chinese video websites such as Youku or Tudou.[36] These websites are the Chinese equivalents of YouTube, while foreign media services including YouTube, Facebook, and Twitter are blocked in China. The viewing numbers for videos on these mainstream websites has exceeded thirty million, and the website of Queer Comrades alone can reach 15,000 per day (Wei Xiaogang, interview, May 29, 2015). For example, Fan Popo's *Rainbow Mama* (2012), a documentary about mothers and their gay and lesbian children, attracted 100,000 views through video websites such as Youku and 56.com before it was taken down in December 2014.

In recent years, LGBT-themed videos have been flourishing online. Among them are the reality webisode series *Gay Lab Show* (*gaoji shiyanshi*, 2014–), the sitcom video series *Rainbow Family* (*yiwu zanke*, 2014–), and the podcast *Gay Lab Report* (*gaoji shiyan baogao*, 2013–). The proliferation of online audiovisual products is also reflected in the decline of website views for Queer Comrades since around 2009. There was a time when one video could achieve 100,000 views in one day, but now there is an increasing number of videos available via various LGBT websites. The censorship has also tightened in recent years as some popular videos were taken down by major video websites, which is allegedly instructed by SAPPRFT (State Administration of Press, Publication, Radio, Film, and Television). One example, mentioned above, is *Mama Rainbow* (2012), which was taken down from video websites in 2014.[37] Apart from video streaming sites, social networking platforms have also been instrumental to queer activism in China. Similar to the feminist activism explored in chapter 1, social media such as Weibo have played crucial roles in disseminating hyperlinks of queer-themed videos online.

An empirical study by Gareth Shaw and Xiaoling Zhang has found that hyperlinks to queer videos uploaded onto video-sharing websites are more widely shared on social networking platforms such as Weibo than on NGO-sponsored websites.[38]

Besides online distribution, *Comrade Yue* is also shown in various contexts offline. In addition to being shown in queer subcultures highlighted by Beijing Queer Film Festival or China Queer Independent Films screenings, the video is also used to organize more grassroots community gatherings, particularly in second or third tier cities. As film screening is usually regarded by authorities as a cultural event and thus less political, the circulation of videos like *Comrade Yue* offline are increasingly a crucial part of community-building. Offline screenings for videos produced by Queer University such as *Brothers* (2013) and *Magic* (2015) are particularly important, as they cannot be uploaded online at full length for reasons of privacy and sensitive content. *Magic* (2015), for example, another documentary produced by Queer University, presents the everyday life of two female-to-male (FTM) transgender sex workers in Shandong Province (Figure 3.3). Queer University student Michael Liu, a volunteer in a local AIDS-related NGO, cross-dresses in real life with his filmmaking subjects. A short trailer is accessible online, but off-line screening events are important for these films.

Twenty to thirty screenings are held in various cities every year. As explained by Wei Xiaogang, the Queer University project is more than a medium to disseminate information and is rather "a platform for creation." For BGHEI, the Queer University project fits into the activist agenda of BGHEI, which took place after 2010. When Xiaogang participated in the 4th Regional Conference in Surabaya, Indonesia in March 2010 organized by ILGA-Asia, the Asian branch of ILGA International Lesbian, Gay, Bisexual, Trans, and Intersex Association (ILGA), the conference was forced to cancel because local religious groups were protesting outside of the conference hotel and many of the participants had to flee. This particular experience led to a shifting of content programming onto Queer Comrades, and the website's focus moved from lifestyle to more attention to rights-related issues. These workshops are similar to what Faye Ginsburg has called "cultural activism" in describing how

Figure 3.3. The poster for *Magic* (directed by Michael Liu, 2014). Image courtesy of Beijing Gender Health Education Institute.

Indigenous and minority peoples use a range of media to respond to "structures of power that have erased or distorted their interests and realities."[39] In this process, video-making itself becomes a personal as well as communal act of coming out through different modes of audiovisual construction. Video is a vital medium to work through and within the processes of identification and community formation.

Queer Becoming as Undoing Heteronormativity and Homonormativity

Besides *Comrade Yue*, other shorts produced in Queer University manifest a great variety of themes and styles that depart from the Direct Cinema style privileged in early films in the New Documentary Movement. These shorts are provocative and challenge the idea of normalcy, or heteronormativity, that sees sexuality as compulsory heterosexuality.[40] Specifically, *Breaking News from a Homosexual China* (*shendu baodao*, 2014) mocks heteronormativity by deploying an interesting twist on the convention of news reporting. In China, although programs are increasingly commercialized in genres such as TV drama and reality TV shows, news reporting remains highly formulaic, as journalism is still seen as the "mouthpiece of the Party" in the state-owned television industry. Under the supervision of the State Administration of Press, Publication, Radio, Film, and Television (SAPPRFT), news reporting in China remains highly censored, and propaganda conventions persist. Every night at 7:00 pm since January 1, 1978, CCTV (China Central Television), China's national TV station, has aired the news program *Xinwen Lianbo*, which has maintained a consistent official reporting style for more than thirty years. Many provincial TV stations must air this program as well, and the program has maintained high ratings nationwide. To resist the conventions of TV journalism, early works of the New Documentary Movement departed from these conventions. Most TV journalism programs, in particular "special topic programs," rely heavily on voice-over narration that interprets the images and events on screen. In contrast, a Direct Cinema style with minimal voice-over is used in many early works by filmmakers such as Wu Wenguang, Duan Jinchuan, and Jiang Yue.

Departing from these earlier aesthetic choices, *Breaking News from a Homosexual China* mocks investigative journalism by reporting heterosexuality as a new "social phenomenon" emerging in Chinese society. Using footage of real news reportage with dubbed voice-overs, the video shows journalists "discovering" heterosexuality. The short film stages an interview with a lesbian couple on the street voicing their concerns regarding the "strange" phenomenon, and with an expert who presents possible theories and statistical data on how heterosexuality came to be, revealing the mechanism of compulsory heterosexuality as well as the specific TV journalism conventions that reinforce it. This short video can be seen as a sarcastic mocking of heteronormative media culture from a point of view of and for the queer community.

Besides challenging heteronormativity, these short films also negotiate with a new gay-dominated cyber culture that reflects what Lisa Duggan has critiqued as homonormativity in the context of neoliberalism. China's Criminal Law in 1997 removed the category of "hooliganism," which was previously used to punish same-sex intimacy between men. In 2001, China's health authorities eliminated homosexuality from the list of mental disorders. In this context, gay-oriented media platforms such as websites and social media flourished. However, gay men dominate cyberspace in China.[41] As I will explain in more detail in chapter 5, these media platforms are increasingly commercialized. Danlan, for example, a major Chinese website for gay users, has attracted millions of users online. In collaboration with the Beijing Center for Disease Control and Prevention, Danlan has launched a series of services besides its website, including Blued, a gay men's social app modeled on Jack'd that has generated investment of around four million US dollars. More recently, social websites and apps such as Zank and Blued have also started to produce online videos. These videos focus exclusively on middle-class or upper-middle-class lifestyles in an urban setting, with little reference to the countryside or migrant workers in the city. Most of the main characters in these videos speak in Mandarin, the official language, and occasionally English as a touch of cosmopolitanism. In contrast, as previously mentioned, in *Comrade Yue*, the image and the accented voice-over create tension in the scene that captures Yue working outside the coal-mining field. While the image shows him physically entrapped by heavy and repetitive labor, his voice-over expresses his strong desire to establish another career and, as I have argued, comments on the lack of social mobility in contemporary China. In the case of *Comrade Yue*, Yue's working-class background is poetically presented and central to understanding his life. Here, the social self or selves constructed in the video intersect with issues of class and other social categories and renders queer becoming an ongoing project of undoing heteronormativity as well as homonormativity.

The sponsorship of *Comrade Yue* is an effort made by the Queer University video workshop to elucidate how sexuality intersects with issues of class, gender, ethnicity, and other aspects of identity. Queer University project also tries to enlarge understanding of sexual diversity through curriculum design and student recruitment. The curriculum combines an introduction to LGBT movements, gender/sexuality, feminist theory, film aesthetics, cinematography, editing, video production and management, and relevant film screenings. Also, Queer University strives to recruit students from different backgrounds and geographical locations, especially those with lower incomes and those who identify as transgender. Among the twelve students in 2014, for example, three students were from smaller cities rather than provincial capitals. Moreover, one participant came from Tibet and another from Chongqing, a city in central-western China. About half of the participants lived in non-coastal areas that are less economically developed.

Conclusion: Queer Becoming as Assemblage

Throughout this chapter, I use the aesthetics of queer becoming to describe how community-based queer videos such as *Comrade Yue* operate as an articulation of identity that intervenes in the ongoing discursive debate between the biological determinist and social constructionist views on homosexuality. At the same time, video-making itself becomes an act of coming out, and video is a vital medium to work *through and within* the entangled process of identification and community formation. It illustrates the logic of assemblage and entanglement between technology and queer expressions in digital masquerade. More importantly, the social self and selves constructed in the video intersect with issues of class and other social categories and render queer becoming as a project of undoing heteronormativity and negotiating with homonormativity. It is in this sense that the aesthetics of queer becoming could be understood as what Kara Keeling calls the "Queer OS"[42] that we explained in the introductory chapter, in which "Queer OS" involves a queer operating system "at the interfaces of queer theory, new media studies, and technology studies." Here, "queer" not only entails non-normative identities but also an "orientation" that negotiates with and questions social norms that are entangled with media technology.[43] The medium of the video, with its capacity for dissemination online, functions as a unique format that gives rise to a new set of queer aesthetics and politics through first-person audiovisual constructions. Nevertheless, the notion of queer becoming does not suggest a teleological and linear progression that arrives at an end product or "complete" identification. Rather, it is a process of queer becoming rather than becoming queers, in which the formation of individuals and communities, and the configuration of audiovisual forms are mutually constitutive. Such an entangled relationship between technology, in this case the digital video medium, and the formation of personal and collective expressions, demonstrates the formation of digital masquerade with the aesthetics of queer becoming. While this chapter charts the production background and the textual features of these queer expressions, the following chapter looks at the exhibition spaces of these digital films, particularly in queer film festivals in Asia, to consider film festival organizing as masquerade.

4

Networking Asia Pacific

Queer Film Festivals and Rights

While the previous chapter theorizes the "aesthetics of queer becoming" as a kind of digital masquerade, this chapter considers queer film festival organizing as masquerade. Situating film festival organizing in an inter-Asia context, I look at the inter-referencing practices of film festival organizing. The notion of inter-referencing has received considerable scholarly attention lately as a critique of Eurocentrism and America-centrism in knowledge production. As Dipesh Chakrabarty acutely points out, the dominance of "Europe" in the production of historical knowledge results in "[t]hird-world historians feel[ing] a need to refer to works in European history; historians of Europe do not feel any need to reciprocate."[1] To counter such a tendency, in *Asia as Method*, Chen Kuan-Hsing calls for "using Asia as an imaginary anchoring point" to allow societies in Asia to "become one another's reference points, so that the understanding of the self can be transformed, and subjectivity rebuilt."[2]

The new millennium has seen a growth of scholarship on inter-Asian connections and comparisons. Chua Beng Huat terms this growing tendency among scholars to make comparisons between locations in Asia "inter-Asian referencing."[3] Aihwa Ong sees "inter-referencing" Asia as a wide range of "practices of citation, allusion, aspiration, comparison and competition" among various Asian urban planning and political practices.[4] Similarly, Chua Beng Huat regards inter-Asian referencing as "actual practices in governance and enterprise in Asia."[5] He discusses how several Asian economies followed in the footsteps of Japan's export-oriented industrialization; how Bangalore, Surabaya, and Dalian learned from Singapore's urban planning; and how Japanese and Korean dramas have been imported into Asian regions with large ethnic-Chinese populations.

According to Chua, this epistemic shift of inter-Asian referencing de-westernizes knowledge production and disrupts the "temporally hierarchical Asia-Euro-America comparison."[6] Following Chua's observations, in this chapter, I look at Asia-Pacific queer film festival networks as practices of inter-Asian referencing, as exemplified by the establishment of Asia Pacific Queer Film Festival Alliance (hereafter APQFFA), to extend the discussion on queer media and rights in China. APQFFA was founded with the aim to increase the visibility of Asia-Pacific queer cinema in 2015. Up until 2018, it was comprised of twenty-three festival members that included queer film festivals in East Asia, South Asia, Southeast Asia (Jakarta, Hong Kong, Seoul, Taipei, Tokyo, Hanoi, Mumbai, Beijing, etc.) as well as cities in Australia, New Zealand, and Hawai'i.

APQFFA epitomizes an emergent field of intensified inter-Asian cultural exchange and collaboration, especially in the queer film festival scene. Moreover, this queer film festival network is based in Asia and extends to the Pacific Islands. As Lisa Yoneyama points out, when a certain space "has been constituted as an object of knowledge and nonknowledge," it is important to "scrutinize the moment of its emergence and consider the interventions and contestations it may reveal or conceal."[7] Thus, it is crucial to ask, what gave rise to this Asia-Pacific network of queer film festivals? What are the possible interventions or limitations? And most importantly, how can it shed new light on the existing analytical framework of inter-Asian referencing and transpacific studies as well as film festival studies?

Film festival studies is a fast-expanding field of academic inquiry with a proliferation of publications in the new millennium.[8] In an overview of the field, Marijke de Valck and Skadi Loist characterize film festivals as "sites of intersecting discourses and practices."[9] Examining these diverse discourses and practices, existing literature has focused on film festivals' programming and selection processes;[10] business;[11] institutional structure;[12] media and audience reception;[13] spatial politics related to issues such as nationhood, city branding, and globalization;[14] and interconnected network.[15]

In particular, "network" has been a crucial framework in the study of film festivals. Thomas Elsaesser's and Marijke de Valck's "international film festival network" model has been influential in the field.[16] Developed from Bruno Latour's actor-network theory, this model sees film festivals as nodal points in a larger cinema network that includes human and non-human actors as well as the "relational interdependence" among these actors.[17] De Valck also uses theories of social interaction, such as Niklas Luhmann's "autopoetic" (preservation of the system) system theory, to understand the film festival network as a self-contained system that uses a few input/output channels to interact with the larger environment. This approach to seeing film festivals as network is also inspired by Manuel Castell's idea of "network society," which describes the spread of networked, digital information technology.[18] Network society gives rise to a new order of global space economy, where the "space of flows" replaces the "space of places" as the dominant logic for social organization.[19] Films, talent, and capital flow through the film festival network.

Scholars studying film festivals have tended to use the concepts of network, flow, interaction, and connection to describe the interdependent relationships among different human and non-human actors. Yet less attention has been paid to how these networks contribute to the politics of power imbalance or hierarchy. For example, actor-network theory cannot explain the "neo-colonial tendencies" in the festival network that influence world cinemas through cultural legitimization, funding availability, and taste making.[20] Accredited, or A-list, film festivals hold the power to "legitimize films and filmmakers." At the same time, they belong to a "self-referential" system that relies on but also helps to produce "new trends, new authors, and fresh new waves."[21]

This chapter examines the politics of inter-referencing through the film festival network of APQFFA. On one hand, I investigate the inter-referencing practices of the film festival network and draw attention to how the hierarchical spatiotemporal constructions in such practices complicate the understanding of inter-referencing as citation, collaboration, and competition. On the other hand, I use inter-referencing to further the discussion of spatial politics in film festival studies. Thinking about the film festival network in terms of practices of inter-referencing, rather than as a pre-given system, points to its frictions and differential formations. Specifically, after contextualizing the proliferation of queer film festivals in Asia, I look at how APQFFA enacts inter-referencing in a way that simultaneously interrupts and reinforces how spatiotemporal hierarchy is currently imagined. In particular, I examine how the network opens up the issue of indigeneity in the Pacific, generating a kind of inter-referencing beyond Asia, while at the same time reflecting the temporal constructions of queer rights. Then I reconsider film festival organizing as a mode of masquerade for its potential ability to disrupt dominant spatiotemporal constructions.

Asia Pacific Film Festival Network as Inter-Asian Referencing

The history of lesbian and gay film festivals in Asia can be traced back to the 1970s.[22] Around 1990, LGBT and queer film festivals started to emerge in various Asian cities. Among them are Hong Kong Lesbian & Gay Film Festival (1989), Rainbow Reel Tokyo (1992), Mardi Gras Film Festival in Sydney (1989), and Melbourne Queer Film Festival (1991). In the 2000s, LGBTQ-themed film festivals proliferated across East Asia, Southeast Asia, and South Asia.[23] The rise of these film festivals coincided with various legal, social, and cultural changes in Asia. Homosexuality was decriminalized in several Asian countries in the 1990s and 2000s. The blossoming of grassroots LGBT social movements in Asia intersected with the increasing involvement of international nongovernmental organizations—such as International Lesbian and Gay Association (ILGA), Ford Foundation, European Union, Oxfam, and Amnesty International—in sexual health and rights in Asia. At the same time, urbanization, the attendant new infrastructure, and the development of creative industries also contributed to the rapid growth of film screenings in venues ranging from multiplex theaters and gallery spaces to coffee shops, restaurants, and bars.

Queer film festivals in Asia have expanded very quickly over the past two decades, and cities such as Seoul and Shanghai now have more than one queer-themed film festival. The development of LGBT film festivals is oftentimes associated with grassroots social movements with specific political agendas for social change and gender and sexual diversity.[24] The proliferation of queer film festivals in the 2000s and 2010s intersected with the rapid growth of grassroots activism and provided a platform for exhibiting a wide range of queer films, including documentaries and shorts. As I explained in chapter 3, the development of digital technologies has also facilitated community-based media production and circulation. In particular, digital video has become a vital medium to work through and within the process of individual identification and community formation.

The emergence of gay and lesbian film festivals in Asia coincided with a global proliferation, professionalization, and specialization of film festivals and the rise of a global film festival network since the 1980s.[25] For many audiences in Asia, knowledge about the queer cultures and histories of other Asian countries is usually routed through Europe or North America. In the 1990s, many of the representative works of queer Asian cinema, such as Ang Lee's *The Wedding Banquet* (1993) or Wong Kar-wai's *Happy Together* (1997), would premiere in major international film festivals before being distributed to other South or Southeast Asian countries. It was through international film festivals in Cannes, Berlin, Venice, Toronto, and Amsterdam that the audience in an Asian country learned about the queer cinema in other Asian countries. This is still the pattern of distribution for contemporary queer Asian cinema, as it is a fast way to successfully reach international as well as Asian audiences. However, the themes and styles of these movies cater to the taste and criteria of the international film festival network, with an emphasis on auteurs and distinctive art cinema aesthetics.

The networking among film festivals in Asia can be traced back to a much earlier period. For example, launched in 1957, the Asian Film Festival, an annual event of the Federation of Motion Picture Producers in Southeast Asia, was held in different Asian cities with an anti-Communist agenda.[26] In the post-Cold War era, film festivals have become a strategy of city branding and attracting tourists. Many key film festivals in Asia (e.g., Hong Kong, Busan, Yamagata, and Singapore) rely on and facilitate inter-Asian connections.

Besides organizing city-based film festivals, film festivals across Asia have also built networks and alliances among themselves. The Network for the Promotion of Asia Pacific Cinema, for example, was founded in 1990 to promote Asian films and filmmakers, particularly in South Asia and Southeast Asia. Established in 2009, the Network of Asian Women's Film Festival (as of 2013) comprised six women's film festivals from India, Thailand, Israel, Japan, South Korea, and Taiwan.[27] Among them are long-term regional actors such as Tokyo International Women's Film Festival, established in 1985, and Women Make Waves Film Festival in Taiwan and SEOUL International Women's Film Festival, founded in

1993 and 1997 respectively. Notably, Women Make Waves in Taiwan has a thematic program section on queer cinema every year, which remains an important platform to showcase feminist queer films and videos.

Compared to these inter-Asian film festival networks established at an earlier time, APQFFA is probably the first cultural network to devote itself to fostering the new wave of queer cultural production and circulation in Asia. APQFFA can be seen as a self-conscious inter-referencing project of networking via its vision, programming, and establishment of a short film showcase and award. First, APQFFA has a collective mission to increase the visibility of Asia-Pacific queer cinema, which is still marginalized in the global queer film scene. According to Jay Lin, the co-founder of APQFFA and the chairperson of APQFFA member Taiwan International Queer Film Festival (TIQFF), "for years as a director and programmer for the Taiwan International Queer Film Festival, I have looked often by default to mostly non-Asian films to fill the line-up, but the reality is that there are many stories originating from the Asia-Pacific that are worthy of sharing with each other."[28] One of the methods APQFFA uses to increase the visibility of Asian stories is to encourage its members to screen films recommended by each other, hence increasing the visibility of films from different countries or regions.

The alliance's inter-referencing practice is also reflected in its emphasis on Asia-Pacific programming via the Asia Pacific Queer Film Festival Alliance Shorts Showcase. In 2017, a special section in the twenty-fourth Mardi Gras Film Festival in Sydney featured films recommended by the alliance members from India, Australia, Pakistan, Taiwan, and China.[29] In the same year, a series of queer-themed shorts was also presented at the Hong Kong Lesbian & Gay Film Festival.[30] Similar programming decisions can be seen in SHPFF in 2018. In August of the same year, the alliance sponsored the Honolulu Rainbow Film Festival (HRFF), which showcased "short films from notable festivals including SHPFF and Rainbow Reel Tokyo."[31] The goal of this showcase was to "disprove the enforced unimportance of Asian characters in media, and the general marginalization of Asian sexuality."[32]

The alliance also established the APQFFA Prize for Best Asian Pacific Short Film to recognize an outstanding short film from the country or region of one of its members. Each festival can nominate one short for competition. In 2016, the award went to the Indonesian short film

The Fox Exploits the Tiger's Might (2015, directed by Lucky Kuswandi, twenty-five minutes), which explores the intimacy between two young boys in a small-town military base. In 2017, the cash award of AUD 2000 was given to *Any Other Day* (2016, directed by Srikant Ananthakrishnan and Vikrant Dhote, twelve minutes), an entry from India nominated by KASHISH Mumbai International Queer Film Festival.[33] The short film shows how two young men are harassed by the police in an everyday setting. In 2018, SHPFF invited and sponsored the filmmaker of *Any Other Day* to visit Shanghai. The short film competition and programming strategies as well as the organization of the visits of festival organizers and filmmakers can be seen as inter-Asian referencing practices. APQFFA facilitates the circulation of these works from one location in Asia to another, without routing through the international film festival network, which is dominated by European and North American film festivals. By doing so, APQFFA provides a platform of horizontal and rhizomatic connections and referencing among different sites across the Asia-Pacific. That the queer festival network is rooted in Asia resonates with what Helen Leung and Audrey Yue call "queer Asia as method," which "highlights practices that decenter the globalized formation of 'queer'; initiates critical conversations on intra-regional cultural flows that are local and international; and provincializes Anglo-American queer knowledge production by revealing its local specificity and non-universality."[34] In the following section of the chapter, I focus on *Lady Eva* (2017), a short film that participated in the APQFFA Shorts program and won the prize in 2018, to demonstrate how the network intervenes in existing geographical imaginations.

Lady Eva: Making Visible the Pacific

Lady Eva is a documentary short about a *leiti* (a Tongan word usually used to refer to a male-to-female transgender person) in Tonga. Selected and recommended by HRFF as part of the APQFFA short film program, the film was screened in several queer film festivals in the network, reaching audiences in Taiwan, Hong Kong, New Zealand, and Japan. It won the Best Short Film Award of the network in 2018. Directed by Dean Hamer and Joe Wilson and produced by Hinaleimoana Wong-Kalu, the documentary follows the story of a *leiti* called Eva Baron. The film provides a rare opportunity for many Asian audiences to learn about transgender issues in the Pacific Indigenous context. The documentary was screened in the Abhimani Film Festival in Sri Lanka and the Quezon City International Pink Film Festival in the Philippines, both of which are members of APQFFA. The documentary feature version of the film, *Leitis in Waiting*, was also featured in Shanghai Queer Film Festival in 2018, and both filmmakers were invited to share their insights with the Chinese audience.

Instead of representing Tonga as "traditional" and "conservative," *Lady Eva* depicts the dynamic activism of *leitis* through the story of Eva Baron. The film begins with a lyrical song accompanying a sequence of montage of typical images of the Pacific Islands—blue ocean and sky, an island with tropical plants, and Indigenous customs and activities. Then the montage segues to Miss Galaxy Queen Pageant Rehearsal on the beach, where *leitis* are wearing their dresses and posing against the beautiful oceanic scenery. Eva recounts her life experience through voice-over in English. She dropped out of school at the age of fifteen and has been working in her family's restaurant as a waitress. Because her family takes issue with her participation in the pageant, she takes refuge in the Tonga Leitis Association office, which also serves as a drop-in center for *leitis*. Eva shows to the camera the interior of the center and introduces pictures of Miss Galaxy on the wall that were taken as early as 1991. Following Eva pointing to the picture of Miss Galaxy 2009, Miss Fatima, the camera cuts to Miss Fatima walking among the audience of the pageant show in 2016. Eva is one of the contestants in the show, and she gives a solo performance imitating Tina Turner. The final sequence of the film shows Eva walking on the stage in slow motion after winning third place and is accompanied by a live singing of "Over the Rainbow." The song, popularized by Judy Garland, has long been appropriated by gay and non-normative sexual subcultures in the American context. At the end of this sequence, the film ends with Eva speaking in Tongan for the first time: "Stand up for yourselves as *leitis*, and your dreams will come true." Here the film shows that the transgender movement in Tonga is taking up ideas such as "rights" to frame their practices, and *leitis* are actively embracing beauty pageant shows under the influence of American popular culture. At first glance, *leitis* singing "Over the Rainbow," instead of songs in Tongan, speaks to the dominance of

American popular culture. Yet the performance on stage can rather be seen as masquerade that is at once submission to the dominance of English and Anglophone pop culture and disruption to the dominant social orders of gender binarism in Tonga.

By visually connecting the exuberant pageant show in 2016 to the pictures on the wall in an everyday setting, the film not only presents the energetic community organizing of *leitis* in contemporary times but also alludes to a much longer history of social activism. Miss Galaxy Queen Pageant has been a fundraising event organized by the Tonga Leitis Association with the mission to advocate human rights and HIV prevention. The drop-in center that Eva uses in the film, the Paea heʻOfa Drop In Centre, opened in 2013, and was supported by Her Royal Highness Princess Salote Mafileʻo Pilolevu. The support from royal members of Tonga challenges the understanding of Tongan culture as conservative and unchanging. The film also demonstrates collaboration among Pacific Islanders, specifically those from Tonga and Hawaiʻi. The film is co-produced by Hinaleimoana Wong-Kalu, a self-identified transgender Native Hawaiʻian, who is also the protagonist of directors Dean Hamer and Joe Wilson's previous film, *Kumu Hina* (2014). *Lady Eva* also received support from a Hawaiʻi-based non-profit organization, Pacific Islanders in Communications.

The circulation of *Lady Eva* through APQFFA highlights the connectedness among the Pacific Islands and other Asian locations. As mentioned previously, APQFFA sponsored HRFF to showcase an Asia Pacific short films collection in 2018.[35] In Hawaiʻi, LGBT-themed movies from Asia are usually routed through major international film festivals such as Sundance, Toronto, Berlin, and Cannes before they reach the queer film festival. Examples of such films include the Thai film *The Iron Ladies* (2000); the Korean films *No Regret* (2006) and *The Poet and the Boy* (2017); the Taiwanese film *Will You Still Love Me Tomorrow?* (2013); and the Japanese film *Close-Knit* (2017). For HRFF, organized by the Honolulu Gay & Lesbian Cultural Foundation, these films are expensive to program, and their aesthetics tend to cater to international art-house film festivals. Shorts or activist films are less likely to be found in this pool of films.[36] In Hawaiʻi, there is "no easy route" to finding films from Asia. As Hamer remarks, APQFFA has enabled filmmakers and programmers to establish contacts with one another and created an alternative "queer film festival circuit" that was not available in the past.[37] The trans-Asia-Pacific network of APQFFA reorganizes the direction of media flow that has been largely structured by the dominant film festival system.

By linking Hawai'i and other Asian cities via showing films such as *Lady Eva*, APQFFA configures a "minor transpacific" cultural network that offers "an alternative regional imaginary and a new referential framework that emphasizes the lateral relations among minor histories and minor locations in the Asia Pacific region."[38] It disrupts the dominant imagination of the Pacific as a region of "economic development and imperial fantasy" by presenting Tonga as a place of active social organizing around issues of sexuality.[39] It also challenges the formulation of "Asia-Pacific" developed and strengthened by traders and military strategists, which fails to capture the transpacific cultural practices at the grassroots level.[40]

The film festival network is inevitably subjected to and conditioned by "scattered hegemonies" across the Asia Pacific, which produce uneven cultural flows and the continuing marginalization of the Pacific Islands.[41] Scholarship on inter-Asian interactions has overwhelmingly focused on economically developed areas, especially East Asia, and the media flows between Japan, Korea, Hong Kong, and Taiwan.[42] Melani Budianta points out that there are more articles on East Asia than Southeast Asia or South Asia published in the journal *Inter-Asia Cultural Studies*.[43] This is certainly due to the economic and cultural dominance and influence of East Asia region. Nevertheless, the journal has made an effort in decentering East Asia, such as by publishing two special issues highlighting the 1955 Bandung Conference in Indonesia (2005) and Third Worldism (2016).[44] Compared to East Asia, South Asia, and Southeast Asia, the Pacific and Pacific Islanders are even more marginalized. As pointed out by Setsu Shigematsu and Keith Camacho, the mainstream usage of the term Asia-Pacific obscures the multiplicity of and the contributions from Pacific Islanders.[45] In his powerful essay "Our Sea of Islands," Epeli Hau'ofa reconceptualizes "Oceania" by evoking the vision that the Pacific Islands are connected, instead of separated, by the oceans.[46] The fluidity of the oceans facilitated migration and exchange across the Pacific long before European migration and settlement.[47] Hau'ofa's formulation of Oceania has significant implications for linking

Asian studies and Indigenous studies by highlighting the connectedness of Asia and the Pacific.

While the Inter-Asian Cultural Studies project represents a "decolonial turn"[48] in knowledge production, the inter-Asia framework is not usually discussed in relation to another decolonizing intellectual endeavor, namely Native/Indigenous studies. By Native/Indigenous studies, I am referring to a diverse body of work that engages with issues of indigeneity and settler colonialism such as Jodi Byrd's (2011) book *The Transit of Empire: Indigenous Critiques of Colonialism* or journals such as *Settler Colonial Studies*. As I point out elsewhere, although scholars who work on Asia and Indigenous studies have both critiqued the epistemic structure of queer studies for particularizing the non-West, and thus are supporting the domination of the West, they are not always in dialogue.[49] In the past decade, more works have emerged to examine the hegemonic power that operates across the Pacific, connecting sites in Asia and the Indigenous concerns within the empire. For example, Vernadette Gonzalez has shown how tourism and militarism have worked in tandem in Hawai'i and the Philippines, where US military modes of mobility and control enable scenic tourist byways, and how in turn, modern tourist consumption reinforces US military dominance.[50]

The transpacific engagements of APQFFA, especially its inclusion of the Wairoa Maori Film Festival and HRFF, open up the potential for such a dialogue. In this light, APQFFA and the circulation of *Lady Eva* within the network point to a model that shifts from "Asia-Euro-America comparison" to transpacific inter-referencing. Such transpacific inter-referencing has the potential to unsettle the existing binary of West/non-West or white/Indigenous and gestures towards an alternative regional imagination that links, in particular, the non-West and the Indigenous.

Queer Rights Discourse and Its Discontents

Exemplifying the practice of inter-referencing in a transpacific context, *Lady Eva* points to the potential of interrupting existing geographical imaginaries. However, it may at the same time run the risk of reinforcing the temporal narrative of queer rights discourse. For example, *Lady Eva* and its sister film *Leitis in Waiting* have been viewed through a homonationalist lens that reifies Tonga as a "conservative" country,[51] or "one of the most conservative and religious places in the world" that marginalizes gender non-conforming people.[52] Such reification reaffirms the purported rights-endorsing liberal tolerance of the West. Film festivals are sites of articulating the contested concepts of women's rights and queer rights. Women's and queer film festivals in Asia often frame their missions and activities in terms of rights, and individual films are also often concerned with equal rights, queer rights, and women's rights, to name just a few. For example, TIQFF collaborated with 1905 Human Rights Film Festival in 2018. The China Women's Film Festival, started in 2012, is one of the women's film festivals based in China. One of the aims of this festival is to address the "issue of rights defense [*weiquan wenti*] faced by women in China and abroad."[53] The festival showcases films produced by women, films with female leads, and stories with women's experience as their thematic concern. These organizations, events, and activism have all used the language of rights to frame their efforts in advancing the social status and well-being of women, sexual minorities, and gender nonconforming people.

APQFFA also frames their activities in relation to queer rights. In October 2017, TIQFF hosted three APQFFA Film and Culture Forums as special events alongside its screening program of 53 films across three cities in Taiwan. The themes of the forums were East Asia and Confucian culture; South/East Asia and the cultures of multiple ethnicities and multiple religions; and Pacific Islanders and Indigenous cultures. The speakers were queer film festivals organizers and/or filmmakers from diverse geographical locations across the Asia-Pacific, including Pakistan, Myanmar, Hawai'i, Australia, Singapore, Hong Kong, Japan, and China. The forums covered a wide range of issues including how the history of colonialism impacts Indigenous queer cultures, racial politics and formation, and queer politics and culture, especially the organizing of queer film festivals in different contexts. Although the different struggles for queer people across the Asia Pacific are lumped together as an "equal rights revolution" in the official discourse, the queer rights discourses and practices discussed in the forums were far more diverse.[54]

In the vast literature on human rights, critical human rights studies and the studies of rights-based feminist and queer social movements are pertinent to examining rights as articulated in queer film festivals. As I pointed out in the introduction chapter, on the one hand, studies on the vernacularization of women's rights and rights-based queer movements have stressed the usefulness of rights discourse. On the other hand, critical human rights studies have analyzed the problematic tendencies in the ideas of human rights, women's rights, and LGBT rights. In particular, what I call the "liberal paradigm critique" points out that the liberal understanding of queer human rights may run the risk of turning homosexuality and gender nonconformity into "an object of consumption and a site of political manipulation."[55]

In this context, though the transparent documentary style in *Lady Eva* presents the vigorous social activism in Tonga, the interpretations of the film could be *overdetermined* by the regime of queer rights, particularly its progressivist narrative. This is similar to the "liberal paradigm critique" I raised in the beginning of this book in the interpretation of Li Tingting and Teresa's wedding. While the APQFFA Film and Culture Forums were framed as an "equal rights revolution," we need to ask whose equal rights revolution it is, and whether or not it projects a temporal narrative based on a hierarchical arrangement of geographical places. In other words, the "liberal paradigm critique" is quite valid in transnational circumstances, especially in light of the spatiotemporal politics of inter-referencing. This linear progressive regime of queer rights is not unlike the dominance of American popular culture exemplified in the singing of "Over the Rainbow" in *Lady Eva*. Again, if we use the term masquerade to look at the use of rights discourse surrounding the film *Lady Eva*, the film should not be overdetermined by the "liberal paradigm critique" on queer rights. Rather, thinking about both the "Over the Rainbow" performance and the use of rights discourses as masquerade enable us to see both the limitation and the potential of transgender activism in the form of digital video. In the next section, I will turn to the exhibitions of these digital videos. Specifically, I focus on film festival organizing as masquerade to illustrate what the "liberal paradigm critique" may not necessarily see.

Film Festival Organizing as Masquerade

During my field research in Taipei in 2015, I attended a panel in the ILGA-Asia conference, featuring the then newly established APQFFA and the organizers from its member festivals. When asked about the reason behind the underrepresentation of lesbian-themed films in some queer film festivals within the alliance, one panelist made a comment that lesbian movies are not "high quality" and thus cannot attract large enough audiences. The view that quality for movies is defined only in terms of production value and box office numbers was challenged by an audience member, who also criticized queer film festival programs, in particular the program of TIQFF, for being dominated by gay male content and marginalizing lesbians and other gender and sexual minorities. In his study of three queer film festivals in San Francisco, Hong Kong, and Melbourne, Stuart Richards uses the framework of social enterprise to examine the transition of queer film festivals from community-based organizations to "corporate elite film institutions" in the neoliberal context.[56] He critiques the homonormativity of queer film festival programming through three perspectives: depoliticization and consumerism, the domesticity of sexuality that confines sexuality to the home, and hierarchies of sexual identity. In particular, Richards examines the programming pattern of the Hong Kong Lesbian & Gay Film Festival, a member of APQFFA. He suggests that HKLGFF's "programming is male dominated"; "the festival programmes significantly more Western content than local films" and the "economic value has a significant influence on the festival's content."[57]

Similar observations can be made about TIQFF. Though the festival uses "queer" in its name, commercial American and European films featuring white gay males tend to dominate the screens. Though films such as *Lady Eva* are included in the program, they are only a small part of the programming. Seen in this light, APQFFA is not exempt from a capitalist understanding of the Asia Pacific, as embedded in entities such as the Asia-Pacific Economic Cooperation. But this observation of a commercialized gay male dominated queer cinema and the developmental logic towards a more commercialized form of cinema does not always apply. While many have to negotiate the tension between financial viability and the mission of representing the diversity of the LGBT community,[58] some queer film festivals function as an alternative space to showcase works that are rarely seen in mainstream outlets.[59] When we criticize the transition of queer film festivals from community-based art organizations to corporate institutions promoting homonormativity, as suggested by Richards, we may overlook the heterogeneity of film festival organizing practices that co-exist at the same time. Here I turn to the case of ShanghaiPRIDE Film Festival (SHPFF), a member of APQFFA, to illustrate this point.

Instead of marching publicly on the street, ShanghaiPRIDE consists of a series of cultural activities in arts, drama, music, sports, and forums. ShanghaiPRIDE started in 2008, and it launched its film festival program in 2015. In 2018, SHPFF lasted for about three weeks, with screenings and events scattered throughout various semi-public spaces such as foreign consulates, gallery spaces, coffee shops, bars, and restaurants across the city. None of the screenings took place in a commercial movie theater. Around the same time of SHPFF in 2018, *Love, Simon,* a 2018 American romantic comedy about the coming-of-age and coming out of a teenage gay man, was shown in the Shanghai International Film Festival, a large-scale state-sponsored film festival. There were six screenings of the film in commercial multiplex theaters belonging to cinema chains located in new and upscale shopping malls. The tickets for *Love, Simon* sold out quickly. This was several months after *Call Me by Your Name* (2017) had been pulled from Beijing International Film Festival. The inconsistent censorship measures imposed on queer films reflect the constraints of state-sponsored large-scale film festivals in China, which are more concerned with their legitimate status as well as city branding and accreditation.[60] While homosexuality is censored in official film productions in China, these official festivals want to attract audiences with critically acclaimed films, some of which involve queer content. However, the accreditation mechanisms governing these official film festivals in China compromise the quality of their programs,[61] as their programming is restricted by official policies regarding import quota and censorship.[62] Networking and marketing are prioritized over the content of the program.[63] Indeed, the business side of these festivals sustains the festivals themselves.[64] In this context, for SHPFF, APQFFA offers a transnational network for alternative film circulation and exhibition that is outside the official film festival system.

On a Monday night during my fieldwork on SHPFF in 2018, I went to a restaurant and bar for a screening publicized in the official social media account of the festival a week earlier. When I walked in, the space was rather empty. The staff told me that the venue of the film screening and event had been changed as the police had put pressure on the owner of the restaurant to cancel the event. Luckily, I was able to look up the new venue online and hurried to the new location several blocks away. Walking through an alley, I finally saw the new place, a Malaysian restaurant and bar. The film screening was taking place at the bar on the second floor. When I walked in, the bar was quite crowded, even though the images projected on the wall were slightly distorted. Later I realized that a festival volunteer had been holding a mic to amplify the sound from the projector throughout the movie. The movie being screened was an Australian production titled *Pulse* (2017). It is about a disabled gay high school student whose consciousness is transported to an abled female body. After the screening, a Shanghai-based activist with a hearing disability shared his experience in LGBT as well as disability activism. Not every screening I attended in SHPFF was as dramatic as this one. Many of the other screenings I went to showed films on bigger screens with decent sound output. But the experience of this Monday night captured the enthusiasm of the organizers and volunteers as well as audiences.

As TIQFF is the main organizer behind APQFFA, usually the annual meeting of the alliance takes place during the film festival. Organizers of other queer film festivals and filmmakers from other parts of Asia gather in Taipei. Ting, one of the organizers of Shanghai Queer Film Festival and SHPFF in 2017, compared the situation in Shanghai and Taipei during her visit to TIQFF:

> The Taiwan International Queer Film Festival is very well-organized. They show films in commercial venues with professional screening equipment. It is different from what we do in Shanghai. In Taiwan, the audience come to watch the movie and then leave. It does not feel like an *activity* (*huodong*). In Shanghai, the audience stay behind after the movie and come up to talk to me all the time.[65]

Ting was ambivalent towards TIQFF. On the one hand, she was impressed by the large-scale programming and professional exhibition equipment in commercial multiplex theaters. On the other hand, she cast doubt on the more commercialized format of film festivals. Her use of the term activity, or *huodong*, a word that connotes moves or actions, suggests an understanding of film festival events as anti-institutional and anti-commercial. This comparison between queer film festivals in Shanghai and Taipei can be seen as a moment of inter-Asian referencing and points to the different forms of queer film festival organizing between Shanghai and Taipei.

The queer film festivals in China, including SHPFF, operate without approval from the state. Like many other independent film festivals in China, queer film festivals in China do not submit films to the censorship authorities for approval. Moreover, since the government keeps a close eye on public gathering, screening events face the risk of crackdown. Independent film festivals in China have used different tactics to maneuver state surveillance, including avoiding naming the event as *dianying jie* (film festival),[66] establishing strategic connections with state institutions,[67] aligning with the cultural policy of local government,[68] keeping the schedule of screening discreet,[69] limiting the audience size and even using an outdoor dinner party as a facade to camouflage the screening.[70] In particular, Beijing Queer Film Festival (BQFF) is known for its use of different tactics to circumvent official surveillance,[71] and it has the potential to constitute a public sphere.[72] It is in this context that film festival as activity, or *huodong*, can be understood as a tactic of queer organizing, and a mode of masquerade in China. In his ethnographically rich research on BQFF, another APQFFA member, Hongwei Bao examines how its guerrilla-style film festival organizing "opened up the question of what constitutes a film festival."[73] In comparison with BQFF, SHPFF is only a part of ShanghaiPRIDE, which features more corporate sponsorship in their publicity material, and their activities are housed in more commercial venues such as private galleries, bars, cafes, and boutique hotels. Though some of the screenings are sponsored by foreign consulates that guarantee smooth screenings and discussions, a significant portion of movies are screened in semi-public commercial spaces. In this sense, SHPFF is more likely to be subjected to the critique of homonormativity despite its tense relationship with the state. Nevertheless, the case of SHPFF demonstrates the heterogeneous realities of film festival organizing in Asia, and it points to an anti-institutionalism that renders queer film festivals in China as *huodong*. These reconsiderations of film festival organizing, generated from inter-referencing practices, offer a critique of gay male dominated queer film festivals and the capitalist logic behind their pursuit of profit and financial viability. The act of masquerading from festivals to *huodong* also echo Antoine Damiens's research on small, ephemeral, and minor queer film festivals in the European and North American contexts,[74] which are often overshadowed by more successful film festivals in the Anglophone world.

Furthermore, the differences and diversity of queer film festivals in Asia provide a fertile ground to look at the necessity of inter-referencing. While the Taiwan Queer Film Festival (TQFF) may appear in a small scale when compared to those in the West, such as OutFest or Frameline Film Festival, the comparison between TQFF and SHPFF puts things into perspective. It is only by inter-referencing TQFF and SHPFF that we can better recognize the relatively more developed civil space for queer organizing in Taiwan, as well as the significance of *huodong* as a mode of *masquerade* in organizing. Framing film festival organizing as *huodong* is a form of masquerade to circumvent state censorship in China. It also gestures towards the importance of non-commercial, ephemeral activities, such as forums and discussions that serve as experimental grounds for inter-referencing. For example, as Fan Popo, the veteran organizer of the Beijing Queer Film Festival, reflects, one of the advantages of the alliance is to cross-over to link with other Asian queer film festivals which face similar situations.[75] For example, the queer film festival organizers in Vietnam shared a similar state sanction on LGBT media content and festival organization. In some cases, film screening content must be pre-approved by the state in Vietnam. Inter-referencing is thus about developing inter-relationships among minor players, and using each other as frameworks to apprehend, facilitate, and advance ideas and practices.

Conclusion: Decentering (Queer) Asia

In their book *Border as Method*, Sandro Mezzadra and Brett Neilson expand inter-Asian scholarship by focusing on the "intertwining of cognitive and geographical borders."[76] They envision a kind of critical regionalism that emphasizes "continental drifts and struggles around borders and mobility." By stressing the "continental drifts," they point out that "the West" that is referred to in inter-Asian scholarship is not a whole but "part and parcel of the capitalist axiomatic of modernity."[77] In this light, I hope the inter-referencing of APQFFA that reorients inter-Asian scholarship to the Pacific Islands and the question of Indigeneity can expand and decenter existing studies on queer Asia. It also opens up a way to look at other minor transnational alliance beyond the inter-Asia framework, such as the transnational video activism between China and Africa examined by Hongwei Bao.[78]

As formulated by Audrey Yue, queer Asia as method "moves away from framing queer Asia as a static geographical site and regional imaginary, and argues for 'queer Asia' as a paradigm that not only queers the concept of 'area' but, more significantly, reorients the flows, boundaries, and hierarchy of global queer knowledge production."[79] In this chapter, building on Inter-Asian Cultural Studies scholarship, I use queer networking to examine the politics of inter-referencing that go beyond Asia. As the connection between Pacific studies and Indigenous studies shows, the parameters of Asia do not describe a stable entity. Rather, the geopolitical as well as knowledge production of the region is constantly shaped by multiple forces such as American popular culture's influence and rights discourses, among others.

This chapter enriches existing studies on the interconnectedness of film festivals by illuminating the hierarchical structure of knowledge production. At the same time, this chapter demonstrates how queer film festival networks, as acts of masquerade, simultaneously interrupt and reinforce how geography and regimes of queer rights are imagined. While Chua Beng Huat's conceptualization of inter-Asian referencing "situate[s] local scholarship as part of the global archive and [. . .] add[s] universalising concepts developed in Asia," we need to ask what concepts in Asia are deemed universalizable and what are not, and what kinds of local scholarship are seen as "part of the global archive" and what are not.[80] To ask such questions is to ask who decides what is local and what is global, and what is universalizable or not. In the age of "the rise of Asia," we should be more cautious about how parts of Asia are visibly referenced and others are obscured. By pointing out the multiple spatiotemporal dynamics and hierarchies from the Asia-Pacific queer film festival network, I hope to contribute to a more critical engagement with the new visibilities of Asia.

5

Platform Presentism

Female Same-Sex Intimacy in App Videos

In 2015, the newly launched social networking application targeting queer women, The L (rebranded as Rela from 2016 to 2021),[1] launched its first online video *X-Love*, a nineteen-minute video that was successful in attracting new users to the app. The video itself has notable overseas reception; it has gathered a viewership of two million on YouTube. The video is "light" in two senses: its lighthearted content and its lightness in form. Adding to the myriad same-sex marriage imaginations in feminist and queer articulation, *X-Love* starts with crosscutting between two women talking happily on the phone about getting ready for an upcoming marriage ceremony. It then jumps to a flashback of how they met and developed an intimate relationship, before returning to the present, when the tomboy sees the more feminine character happily in her wedding gown (Figure 5.1). Up to this point, the audience build up the expectation to see a wedding between two women, only to find out that the tomboy is a best man, and the more feminine character is actually marrying a man. Only after this plot twist, which is already halfway into the short film, does this video present the tomboy's perspective of the heartbreaking experience of "losing" the girl to a man. The tomboy, who never directly reveals her feelings to the marrying woman, shares their pictures and her thoughts on the app, The L. When the tomboy runs off from the wedding venue and cries out on the street, another plot twist follows—a bridesmaid from the wedding follows her and stands right next to her. The bridesmaid learns of the tomboy's story through her posts on the app. Instead of talking to the tomboy directly, the bridesmaid sends a greeting on The L on her phone. The tomboy sees her message and her profile pictures on the app, which indicates that the girl is only two meters away. The video ends with the tomboy looking up

Figure 5.1. Screen shot of *X-Love*. Image courtesy of The L.

and seeing the bridesmaid in a soft bright light, illustrating how the app leads to *X-Love*, which stands for an unknown love in the future that is full of possibilities. The second plot twist leads back to the lighthearted tone in the beginning. It is obvious that the video serves to promote the app and promises that the app leads to connectivity with other women who are interested in women romantically.

The lightness of these social app videos is not only about the light-hearted tone of the story, but the "screen dimensions, movie length, and file size."[2] This video, labeled as a les (short for lesbian) micro-film, can be seen as a new development of what Paola Voci calls "portable movies" produced for the mobile phone, which are too amateur to be examined in relation to authorship, film art, and the film industry.[3] *X-Love* is not only lighter in their tone; it is also short in length, which makes it more convenient to watch via the app on the smartphone. *X-Love* exemplifies a wave of micro-films featuring female same-sex intimacy, funded or distributed by lesbian dating apps that started to appear around 2015. These online videos, ranging from a few minutes to feature-length, are generated by lesbian and bisexual women's social networking apps such as The L (Rela). I call the videos produced by and released through the social networking apps "social app videos" not only because they are at least partly funded by the apps but also because a considerable portion of their storylines directly involves the use of the social app. Moreover, these videos are intended to be watched via the app on smartphones before they are released on video sharing sites. These "social app videos," ranging from three to eighty minutes in length, are promoted as micro-films, online movies, or miniseries that are exclusively streamed on the apps before being released on video sharing platforms such as Youku or iQiyi. These social app videos can be seen as examples of "social media entertainment" in an evolving media ecology.[4] Unlike the independent or NGO-sponsored queer works that circulate largely in the community and queer film festival networks mentioned in previous chapters, this new wave of online videos reached considerable size of audience, which is significant as lesbian representation is still a taboo in commercial film and television.

In this chapter, I use the notion of "platform presentism" to theorize the "lightness" of social networking app related videos, both in tone and form, as a key feature of digital masquerade. My definition of platform presentism is twofold. Contextually, platform presentism points to the experimental engagement of the platform that redefines media genres and creates "light" entertainment content that plays around state censorship. Textually, platform presentism marks a shift to lighthearted stories of the present mediated by digital platforms, which departs from previous representations of lesbianism as the mournful past.

Combining interviews with key staff members of social networking apps as well as textual analyses of selected videos, I explore the entangled relationship between platforms, as well as gendered and sexualized social relations through the online videos made by LESDO and The L (Rela)—the social app videos. I will first contextualize the emergence of "social app videos" against the platformization of online video industry below. In this part, I aim to create a dialogue between expanding the field of "platform studies" that emphasizes economic and technical affordance, and the concerns of feminist science and technology studies. Following the notion of digital masquerade, I conceptualize the platforms, specifically social networking apps and video sharing sites in this case, as assemblages of material settings, predispositions, discourses, and practices. Then I will move on to analyze the narrative and aesthetic features of these videos, particularly its platform presentism. Specifically, I look at the community plot in *The L Bang*, an online sitcom series produced by The L, to illustrate the two meanings of platform presentism. In this chapter, I revisit the "liberal paradigm critique," especially Lisa Duggan's elaboration on homonormativity,[5] which is often used to criticize the depoliticizing gay culture that centers around consumption, including the pink economy and the commercialization of LGBT cultures. Recognizing the possible limits of the new lesbian visibility, this chapter gives credit to the new and long-awaited representation of lesbians, without quickly dismissing these trendy videos as upholding middle-class and homonormative values that associate with privileged social groups.

The Platformization of Chinese Online Video Cultures

The new video culture generated via the apps is indicative of a larger convergence of video sharing platforms and social networking platforms, where the video platformization has enabled more flexible modes of video production and distribution. Platforms and platformization, or *pintai* and *pintaihua* in Chinese, have become umbrella terms in business discourse to describe the development of all kinds of websites, apps, and infrastructures in the context of digital entrepreneurship.[6] They speak to the ongoing discussions on "platform economy"[7] and "platform capitalism."[8] The scholarship on digital economy in China is a fast-growing field, oftentimes with a political economy approach, such as the studies on digitized economy,[9] Chinese Internet companies,[10] convergence of telecommunications, broadcast, and Internet networks,[11] digitization of television,[12] social media, and institutionalization of copyright.[13] As I elaborated in the introductory chapter, research on communication technologies in mainland China, particularly media censorship and civic activism, has flourished considerably. More recently, the focus on Chinese platform economy has also expanded into how issues of gender and sexuality are intertwined with the formation of technology and society. In particular, Audrey Yue looks at the Singapore-based gay web portal Fridae as a social enterprise with "illiberal yet pragmatic moral legitimacy"[14] in a country where homosexuality remains criminalized. Denise Tang explores the affective dimension of a Hong Kong-based lesbian dating app Butterfly and Tingting Liu looks at how LESDO function as emerging digital infrastructure that provides community-based care to female queer subjects.[15] The lesbian dating apps, together with other Chinese dating apps, form what Lik Sam Chan has called "emergent publics" in urban China.[16] Building on these recent scholarship, this chapter draws from feminist scholarship to understand platformization in contemporary China. Feminist scholarship on technology has criticized the social and historical forces which limit women's access to technology, and how technology itself is gendered.[17] As I explain in the introduction, feminist epistemology encourages us to recognize the partiality of knowledge as produced through particular subject positions and the entanglement between what is conventionally separated as subject and object. Thus, the studies of technological forms such as interface, code, platform, and computation should not be separated from the analysis of (gender, racial, sexual, and other) differences and power.[18]

In the case of social app videos, the platformized video technology is not autonomous, static artifacts. Instead, they are manifestations of multiple interactions happening across people, practices, and platforms. Moreover, how can the "platformization" of Chinese society renew current feminist discussions on technology? This chapter answers these questions by focusing on the temporality of social media. Social media and other digital platforms are said to be creating a sense of time that privileges the present by absorbing the "unoccupied time" through engaging users with a myriad of online architecture.[19] In contrast to the standardized clock time, digital media engenders "network time" in the virtual world, which is defined by the ever-increasing acceleration of computer development.[20] These observations about the temporality of social media seem to affirm the notion of high-speed societies shaped by digital technologies.

However, in her book *Pressed for Time: The Acceleration of Life in Digital Capitalism*, Judy Wajcman questions this premise through understanding the co-constitution of technology and society from the perspective of feminist science and technology studies.[21] For Wajcman, temporal qualities such as instant connectivity are not inherent in machines; they must be generated through human engagement with objects. Perceptions of time do change with new technology, but this change always occurs in a specific cultural and material context.[22] Thus the investigation of the temporality of social media and, in this case, how women's videos imagine and materialize time on (small) screen, must be contextualized.

China's video platforms such as Youku and Tencent Video started as databases of user-generated contents, including pirated or appropriated contents, and later obtained a license for film and television shows to include proprietary traditional media contents.[23] The online video industry in China has been growing rapidly in recent years. The audience of online videos in China reached 514 million in 2016, of which the female audience amounted to 46.9%. Among these users, 95% had experience using smartphones to watch online videos.[24] Various online video platforms such as Tencent, Youku, and iQiyi have started to invest millions of US dollars to buy online rights for notable movies, as well as television drama or reality shows. At the same time, online video productions, including those funded by video-sharing platforms, have grown drastically. In 2016, the State Administration of Press, Publication, Radio, Film, and Television database for online video documented 4430 online series, 4620 online movies (including micro-films), and 618 online variety shows.[25] This number excluded user-generated content (UGC) videos. The changing mediascape of online videos or platformization of online videos provided a fertile ground for social app videos to appear.

Besides the economic context of online video industry, the popularity of the "social app videos" is also caused by the asymmetrical mediascape of China, where gay and lesbian content is strictly censored in cinema and on television. Though many LGBT shows and movies from Taiwan, Hong Kong, and other parts of the world enjoy great popularity online, oftentimes through online pirated versions, there has been a lack of domestically produced commercial audiovisual content. That is not to say there is no homoeroticism on screen. Rather, explicitly addressing homosexual sexual acts or characters who identify as homosexuals or nonnormative gendered persons is quite recent.[26] In the 1990s, as mentioned in chapter 3, fictional films such as Chen Kaige's *Farewell My Concubine* (1993) and Zhang Yuan's *East Palace West Palace* (1996) received critical attention, yet these more acclaimed films have less relevance to contemporary gay lives. Li Yu's *Fish and Elephant* (2001) is arguably the first lesbian feature film from mainland China. These feature films are usually seen as art movies or underground cinema, which limits their accessibility to the general public. With the wide accessibility of digital camcorders at the turn of the twenty-first century, various independent videos and documentaries engaging with LGBT issues emerged[27] and represented a variety of queer bodies.[28] This new body of what Helen Leung calls "new Chinese queer cinema"[29] is made up by a varieties of commercial as well as independent films and videos, including self-identified queer filmmakers such as Cui Zi'en, Shitou, and later Fan Popo, who are also key figures in the booming LGBT activism and community-building since the early 2000s.

In the 2010s, feminist and queer activists creatively used websites and social media to spread queer-friendly community-based videos. These projects produced hundreds of short videos, giving rise to a new set of queer aesthetics and politics through first-person audiovisual constructions, and at the same time problematizing queerness rather than simply affirming homosexuality.[30] Empirical evidence showed that social-networking sites and platforms such as micro-blogs have been crucial in disseminating these domestic videos; linking video-hosting platforms to social networking platforms, such as posting Youku links of documentaries on micro-blog, has been an efficient method for marginal groups to reach a wider audience.[31] Apart from state censorship, financial difficulties are often the challenge faced by individual filmmakers and LGBT activist organizations. At the same time, representations of male same-sex intimacy, often in the form of fan fiction or amateur videos, are proliferating online due to a growing interest in Boy Love content that attracts a large audience of women. In comparison, the domestic representations of female same-sex intimacy are disproportionally in short supply.

It is in this context of platformization of online videos and the scarcity of domestic lesbian media content that the social app videos take shape. Social networking startup companies provide previously unimaginable funding for online videos about same-sex intimacy. Comparatively speaking, it is rather rare to see social networking apps so active in producing and distributing videos. Most English-language dating apps have the sole purpose of enabling users to interact on an individual base.

Other dating apps in Asia, such as the Hong Kong-based lesbian dating app Butterfly, has a forum function, but it never expands to video production.[32] In the following section, I explore how the social app videos acts upon "platform presentism," where the experimental engagement with the platform in its evolving present redefines media genres.

Presence of the Platform: A Form of Lightness

The presence and relevance of the platform are realized in multiple ways. First of all, "platform presentism" describes the presence of the platform and its quickly adaptive business model in crossing media boundaries and reinventing media genres. The story of how social app videos appeared is quite telling in this manner. This new wave of social app videos I look at were mostly produced by two social networking or dating apps, Beijing-based LESDO and Shanghai-based The L. Both companies launched the apps in 2012–14, and the names of LESDO and The L (Rela) refer to the term lesbian or *lala*, the colloquial term for lesbians in China. Both companies recognized the importance of providing content, in this case, lesbian-themed videos, as a major feature of the social networking app platform around 2015. Both apps produce lesbian-themed fictional videos or miniseries to attract users by making them available exclusively through the apps before their subsequent release on Youku, iQiyi, or YouTube. Internet video production is one of the key strategies for both lesbian apps to accumulate more than a million users within a year or two. The production of these videos is one of the strategies of the emerging dating app startup culture to actively "produc[e] sociality"[33] for market competition. The videos were successful in accumulating millions of users for the two startup companies, which led to further investment. Following in the footsteps of gay men's dating apps Blued and Zank, LESDO and The L secured further investments and strategic funds in 2016.

In 2015, LESDO secured the online distribution rights of Thai movie *Yes or No 2.5* (2015) and collaborated with iQiyi, a major online video platform. *Yes or No 2.5* is the second sequel of Thai film *Yes or No*, a movie about the romantic relationship between two female university students (Figure 5.2). The first two films were never officially released in theaters or online in China, yet the movie had already built a fan base

Figure 5.2. Promotion material for Thai film *Yes or No 2.5*.

on Weibo and Baidu Tieba. LESDO made this new sequel available initially for free only through the app for a limited period of time before it was made available on iQiyi. On iQiyi, the whole movie had the LESDO logo on the right corner of the screen and thus attracted potential users to the app. According to the data provided by LESDO, the viewership of *Yes or No 2.5* exceeded ten million across all platforms in 2015. The movie drew 350,000 new users who downloaded and registered the app, which was an 80% growth. It also brought considerable profit through splitting advertising venue with iQiyi.[34] After the success of *Yes or No 2.5*, LESDO produced and distributed several online movies in the next two years, including its first micro-film *Always Miss You* (2016, thirty-four minutes) and the online movies *True Love, Wrong Gender* (2016, sixty minutes) and *Girls Who Talk to Flowers* (2016, twelve minutes) (Figure 5.3).

Similarly, The L has produced a variety of videos with different durations and formats, such as the 80-minute road movie *Touch* (2016) (Figure 5.4), as well as micro-films such as *X-Love* (2016, nineteen minutes). The L also makes more efforts in creating series. *The L Bang* (2015), for example, is a four-episode sitcom series portraying the lives of four lesbians and one gay male friend who share the same floor in a high-rise apartment in urban Shanghai. *The Girls on Rela* (2017–), another lesbian

Figure 5.3. Promotion material for *Girls Who Talk to Flowers*.

Figure 5.4. Promotional poster for online movie *Touch*. Image courtesy of The L.

short film series, uses crowdsourcing to develop its content. It recruits real users as actors in the short videos and features interpersonal relationships, including first encounters on the street, long-distance relationship maintenance, relationship developments, and so forth. This crowdsourcing approach to find talents is similar to what Zhao called "professionalizing amateurs."[35] The production team puts together these amateurs' original content on online video sites, solicits input from social media such as Sina Weibo, and incorporates comments from the audience in script development. In this case, the app itself becomes the platform to enhance user interaction and invites users not only to write the script but also act in the videos.

Davis and Xiao have pointed out that one of the distinctive features of platforms in mainland China is how it "combine[s] multiple functions."[36] For example, WeChat, which started as a messenger app, has developed into a self-contained ecosystem that was built on an open-platform architecture combining social media, e-commerce, food delivery, and other services. This could also apply to the understanding of the multiple functions of both lesbian dating apps: combining video entertainment and social networking. Nevertheless, the details of how LESDO and The L tapped into online video production demonstrates the quick adaptability of the app in reinventing itself across traditional media genres. While LESDO uses online film distribution of other Asian films to broaden their user base before producing lengthier online videos, The L is more active in producing a variety of original content, which includes feature-length online videos, web series, and short videos. Social networking applications such as LESDO and The L take the opportunity of video sharing sites' high demand for original content and the relatively loose censorship and regulation environment for online videos. These videos are not necessarily subject to state censorship because they are not feature films or television dramas that need to obtain license or script approval before shooting. Some of the videos that include within their stories the obvious use of their own app, almost fall within the boundary of advertisement or infomercial. This entrepreneurial vision defines the "lightness" of these social app videos, particularly their length and the flexibility of distributing them to channels across different platforms. Apart from the abundance of shorts which only last for several minutes, the predominant length is within half an hour. The feature-length films can also be understood as being part of the flexible strategy employed by the apps. This "lightness" is helpful in navigating the uncertain media environment and censorship. For example, in June 2017, the China Netcasting Services Association issued regulations that sought to ban online content that featured same-sex relationships.[37] *Addiction* (2017), a drama about four gay teenagers, was a major success for iQiyi until it was taken down without explanation.[38] Yet shortly after the censorship of *Addiction*, the aforementioned lesbian-themed *True Love, Wrong Gender* was released and gained 300 million views on Weibo. Here, the platform presentism is evident as the lightness in form (in terms of its short length and flexibility of the distribution channels), which helps out-maneuver the strict media censorship on homosexuality.

Temporal Lightness and Its Discontents

In *Backward Glances*, Fran Martin argues that a temporal logic dominated the representation of female same-sex love in Chinese-language films and media throughout the twentieth century, where female homoeroticism was usually represented as past experiences such as schoolgirl love stories.[39] Such a "memorial mode," especially in works from Taiwan and Hong Kong where homosexuality on screen is less censored, seems to render female same-sex love as having no future and hence denies lesbian possibility. However, the mournful remembrance of same-sex love implies a critique of the "hetero-marital" regulation on adult women.[40] In contrast to the "memorial mode" and the persistence of the past, a majority of the online movies made by the two apps demonstrate platform presentism, a shift to lighthearted stories of the present mediated by digital platforms, which departs from previous representation of lesbianism as the mournful past. Specifically, platform presentism promotes a new form of women's sociality emphasizing connectivity via mobile technology, but it is also conditioned by an urban and consumerist environment. As the geolocative function of social apps provides a browsing experience that focuses on the here and now, it is no surprise that the social app videos predominately center on the current moment. Platform presentism is thus defined by an emphasis on relationality and connectivity that brings new ways of narrative registers, gender expressions, and audiovisual aesthetics. Before LESDO and The L started to produce films, Blued, the major gay men dating app in China, appeared in the Internet short video *My 17 Gay Friends* (2014, twenty-four minutes). This video features seventeen protagonists instead of a main character. The true "character" is the interconnectedness of the seventeen gay men in Beijing. Similarly, connectivity among women remains a central role in the narratives of these videos, which is facilitated by the design of the app.

The design of the app itself popularizes relational self-identity. In the user profile setting section, The L users only need to provide an avatar picture, username as well as ID, and identify their gender roles in a relationship. In 2017, the choices included T, P, H, Bi(sexual), straight, *fujoshi* (a Japanese term describing women who are fans of cultural products depicting male same-sex intimacy), other, and "do not show." T, P, and H are terms describing the secondary genders in female same-sex relationships. T refers to tomboy. P comes from *Po* and, loosely, a tomboy's girl in Taiwan, which usually means a more feminine woman. H usually refers to a lesbian woman who does not identify as T or P but could desire both/either/neither T and/or P. These terms are usually loosely translated into butch, femme, and versatile, respectively. LESDO, in a similar fashion, enables users to indicate an array of gender identities, including T, P, H, Bi(sexual), and confidential. The design of the dating apps forces users to select secondary genders and centralizes the relationality among women.

The emphasis on relationality among women is reflected by its focus on representing female same-sex intimacy and sociality among a wide range of gender expressions of women, particularly androgynous, masculine, or genderfluid women. The intention behind the video production for LESDO is to create a "new image of women" and "*zhongxin* (androgynous)" celebrities in order to reflect "the diversity of love and relationship."[41] Based on analyzing the user reviews of twenty-six Euro-American as well as Asian lesbian-themed movies on Douban, a Chinese social networking website that focuses on film, music, and books, the research team of LESDO found out that many movies were made by male producers and directors, and the characters were performed by straight women. The investigation also concluded that the most popular character type was the "soft butch" who has long hair and displays androgynous gender features.[42] This finding leads to the first micro-film produced by LESDO, *Always Miss You*, to cast a soft butch as one of the main characters.

The mainstream popular image of women in contemporary media is urban, economically successful, fashionable, and sexually attractive, marking a break from the sexless and androgynous woman of the Cultural Revolution era.[43] This woman is portrayed as taking full advantage of the opportunities given to her by market liberalization. However, this idealized image is fraught with the exclusion of women from working-class and rural backgrounds. Moreover, as Evans argues, the emergence of this new image of woman is accompanied by the widespread belief and cultural discourse that the passive woman depends on her active, entrepreneurial husband. The traditional binary concept of gender roles, which subsided during Mao's era, has resurfaced during market reform.[44] This emphasis on femininity and the feminized gender role can be seen as the refeminization of women in popular culture.

The women represented in the social app videos encompasses a range of unconventional gender expressions, from "soft butch" to more masculine ones. In contrast to the sexless androgynous woman of the socialist period who devoted herself to her job and the nation, the new androgynous woman is highly sexualized and expresses female same-sex intimacy and desire. Androgynous women are not rare in Chinese popular culture. Chris Li, who made her name by championing the singing reality show *Super Girl* in 2005, was famous for her androgynous gender expression. However, her androgynous appearance has been toned down after she made her fame. With a higher tendency to display femininity in her publicity pictures, she is sexualized through dressing up in revealing feminine clothes. At the same time, however, she is "desexualized," as she has rarely been paired up romantically with men or women in her music videos or blockbuster movies. In contrast, the social app videos' narrative focuses on relationality and connectivity and offers a different approach to representing androgynous or masculine women.

Along with the representation of a diversity of gender expressions, the social app videos also feature the homoerotic relations surrounding these women. The social app videos aim to portray "realist interactions that are more appealing to lesbians."[45] In particular, the movies tend to portray the gender role of P, usually the more feminine woman,

Figure 5.5. Promotional poster for online movie *True Love, Wrong Gender.*

as more active in the relationship.[46] For example, the online movie *True Love, Wrong Gender* (Figure 5.5) distributed by LESDO tells the story of two college girls sharing a room at school, a setup similar to the Thai film *Yes or No* (2010). In the publicity material of the movie, both actors show their LESDO account to attract audience. The title of the movie implies the conventional social presumption that women who love women have a "wrong" gender. It perpetuates the logic of compulsory heterosexuality, which Adrienne Rich famously coined to describe how heterosexuality is assumed until proved otherwise, and thus reinforced, while marginalizing other sexual orientations.[47] Yet the opening scene of the film depicts the more feminine woman, Xiaorou, taking a peep at the more masculine woman, Miller, in the shower. The extreme close-ups Miller's hair, face, lips, body, and tattoos on her body are shown through point-of-view shots from the conventionally feminine woman. The gaze cast on the butch woman's body is no longer a male gaze[48] but a female gaze in the storyline and through the point-of-view of the feminine female character Xiaorou. The following scene features Xiaorou and Miller making out in bed, ending with a long kiss. In this way, the movie portrays the conventionally beautiful, feminine woman taking a more active role in the relationship. Then the active role of the feminine woman is downplayed when the movie reveals the shower scene and sex scene to be a dream sequence. Nonetheless, the movie features Miller as the irresistible object of desire for Xiaorou later on in the movie as the two of them become romantically involved.

At first glance, the social app videos and their preference on present-time connectivity among women seem completely different from Martin's emphasis on the "memorial mode" as a distinctive characteristic in representing homoeroticism in Chinese culture. One can argue that a lingering "memorial" temporal logic can still be found in some of the "social app videos." The first micro-film produced by LESDO, *Always Miss You* (2016, thirty-five minutes), adapted from an online novel, follows the story of Xue, who travels back in time to three years ago, when she first met her love, Wei. She re-lives her life and hesitates to get to know Wei, fearing that she may not bring happiness to her in a same-sex relationship. Yet the attraction between the two continues to grow despite Wei's hesitation. In the end, Xue falls fatally ill and tries to re-unite with Wei in a virtual world by returning to three years ago. The present is defined by the two women's separation of the physical/virtual world. The present also ends when Xue dies, and the two women, again, have no future. Despite seemingly unfolding the events of the present time in the beginning, the video tells the story of a mournful past. However, unlike the schoolgirl romance that usually ends with the hetero-marriage of one of the characters who reaches feminine adulthood, the mournful past of remembrance in the video, told from a time-travel narrative device, is the remembering of the intensity of the same-sex love and relationship.

Aside from the temporal lightness in the platform presentism and the narrative of relationality, the lightness of the content is reflected in its characterization, plot, and style. In terms of content, the young age of characters, as well as stories about first love and first jobs, suggest that the viewers are predominately young, ranging from teens to twenties. Furthermore, stylistic choices in the videos reflect the production team's assumption that viewers tend to watch the videos on smartphones. For example, close-ups are often used to show the characters' expressions on a small screen. While some of the establishing shots are long or medium shots, the frequent use of close-ups is obvious in many of the social app videos.

Despite breaking new grounds in the social app videos, this new visibility also has flaws. The reliance on self-identity in its narrative of relationality is not without drawbacks. If we take a second look at *X-Love*, the video we discussed in the beginning of this chapter, the woman who is getting married is deemed unavailable in reality and absent in the dating app, though she at one point says to the tomboy that she would marry her if she were a man. The story forecloses a universalized understanding of female same-sex eroticism. It makes the feminine woman purely a friend despite the overtly intimate interactions between the two women. It eventually codes the feminine woman as "straight," and *naturalizes* her choice of entering a heterosexual marriage.

Furthermore, the tendency to focus on young, pretty/handsome, and urban middle-class women has its limitations. The women in the social app videos are predominately young, beautiful, or handsome, dressed up in a cosmopolitan style, and living in an urban environment. Women in the working class and with rural backgrounds are excluded in this context. Moreover, these social app videos feature women who have access to smartphones and mobile apps, excluding those with limited access to the technology. Thus, the representation of female same-sex intimacy in the dating app videos is limited by the platform's own position as an urban-based social network and its promotion of the middle-class lifestyle. As Liu Tingting suggests, rural migrant lesbians actively use digital communicative technology such as QQ group chat to carve out a queer space in their everyday life in the city.[49] Yet this social group is largely absent in the dating app videos. While these videos bring new visibility of gender diversity that features female same-sex connectivity and relationality, they simultaneously endorse an urban middle-class lifestyle that excludes the working class or rural migrant queer women.

This new image of women and lesbianism should also be contextualized in relation to the pink economy in China, or the commercialization of the LGBT movement and sexual diversity. Despite strict media censorship on homosexual content, the LGBT lifestyle has been recognized as a model for the economy, especially in relation to digital entrepreneurship. According to *China Daily*, China's major state-sponsored English newspaper, China is the world's third-largest LGBT market, after Europe and the United States, and is valued at $300 billion per annum.[50] In 2012, Blued, the gay hook-up app, was founded, and it developed so fast that by 2016 it had an estimated value of $600 million. Now it is actively promoting its business overseas and has more daily users than Grindr from United States, making it the largest gay dating app in the world.[51] In this context of the pink economy, The L and LESDO are able to get funding for their apps and the social app videos. The L started its online video business in order to promote the app. It includes micro-movies that feature the brand, coming-out videos to raise public awareness on gender and sexuality, and web series. The initial motivation for both The L and LESDO to tap into online video industry was to create branding awareness and to attract users to the apps.[52] Yet these works are easily circulated and the demand for them is "extremely high" as "the whole market has little gay-themed works." This becomes an advantage for these app videos.[53] In this context, the liberal paradigm critique, specifically Duggan's critique of homonormativity, is helpful in pointing out the inevitable emphasis on consumption in the booming pink economy in China, in which same-sex dating apps play an important role.

Nevertheless, social app videos cannot be considered simply as product placement when they develop into feature-length films or series. If we think about social networking platforms as assemblages of material settings, predispositions, discourses, and practices, social app videos are not only promotional products for the apps but also a discursive formation of imagining female same-sex desires and intimacy. These videos further provide the "scripts" of how the social networking app is immersed in everyday life in various ways. These films, shorts, and series made by the two apps create new conceptions of spatiality and temporalities among women. They are the "networked publicity strategies" of social media platforms that produce new norms of sociality and connectivity.[54] In other words, the liberal paradigm critique may be missing the complexity of the digitized queer articulations. Questioning the universality of Duggan's critique of homonormativity, Ying-Chao Kao's ethnographic study points out that in the context of same-sex marriage campaigns in Taiwan, glocalization of homonormativity theory has generated the disruption between queer theory and embodied experiences.[55] Similarly, despite their limitations, the social app videos and their platform presentism should not be simply dismissed as commercial products for the middle class's taste or reduced to a new homonormativity. Instead, the boundaries between entrepreneurial aspiration and community activism are not mutually exclusive. In the next section, I use the specific example of *The L Bang* to illustrate this complexity.

The L Bang: Platform Presentism and the Community Plot

The L Bang is one of the signature web series produced by The L in 2015. This four-episode sitcom series demonstrates platform presentism in several ways. First, this series' form is light. In terms of length, each episode is short, and there are fewer episodes per season when compared to traditional television drama. Usually, a web drama episode lasts around twenty minutes, instead of the regular forty-five minutes. This production decision is made with the assumption that viewers watch them in environments such as public transport and thus have a shorter attention span.[56] As many of the videos are released via the apps first, mobile devices are the preferred platform for viewing.

Self-styled as a "young urban lesbian light comedy," the lighthearted quality is achieved through its plot. Its lightness is also evident in its "apartment plot" of accidental encounters and quick problem solving. Pamela Wojcik coins the term "apartment plot" to describe a variety of films and television shows that employ the apartment as a central narrative device. Wojcik points out that the apartment plot is a part of a mid-twentieth-century urban American discourse that viewed home through values of community, mobility and visibility, instead of perceiving home as private, family-oriented, and stable.[57] The apartment plot is both a setting and a genre that presents a philosophy of "domestic urbanism," which "mobilizes urban themes inside the home"[58] and "marshal[s] utopian fantasies of neighborhood, community, contact and porousness."[59]

Figure 5.6. Promotional poster for *The L Bang*. Image courtesy of the L.

The L Bang can also be seen as an example of the "apartment plot," where five lesbian, gay, and bisexual characters happen to be living on the same floor in urban Shanghai (Figure 5.6). *The L Bang* is a situation comedy miniseries that is inspired by the online popularity of *Rainbow Family* (2014, 2015), a sitcom series produced by gay dating app Zank. *Rainbow Family*, sponsored by Zank, features the story of three consumption-oriented gay men, one straight man, and a straight woman in a generic middle-class apartment in urban China. Similarly, *The L Bang* online series cleverly uses the social-app mediated "apartment plot" to represent new means of sociality among women in an urban setting by featuring a group of lesbian and bisexual women living on the same floor. Here I use the term "the community plot" to describe how the dating app functions as a central narrative device and visual trope in representing same-sex intimacy in urban interior and exterior settings in videos such as *The L Bang*.

Lee Wallace's book *Lesbianism, Cinema, Space: The Sexual Life of Apartments* points out that stories of lesbianism in American films invariably engage with an apartment setting, a spatial motif not typically associated with lesbian history or cultural representation.[60] The book critiques the theoretical identification of public sex cultures as the basis for a queer counterpublic sphere. In a similar light, I find that *The L Bang*

嗯 今年骄傲节有一场话剧

Figure 5.7. Screen shot of *The L Bang* depicting the main characters participating in the community event ShanghaiPRIDE. Image courtesy of The L.

contributes to an urban discourse and imagination that center on community and visibility, in this case a lesbian community facilitated by the social networking platform. In the first episode, the encounter between the main characters is facilitated by the app when one of the characters suspects that their neighbor is also a user of The L, based on their proximity suggested by the app, as well as the similar view from the apartment window shown in her photo sharing on The L. A lot of character interactions are facilitated by the app, which serves as a narrative device linking the characters together and the visual trope that occupies the center of the screen. In addition to developing the story in the domestic setting of the apartment, the characters in the show also use the app to connect with the organizers of ShanghaiPRIDE, an important LGBT community event, and the organizer of ShanghaiPRIDE film festival discussed in the previous chapter. In one of the scenes, Aisha, a character who is interested in becoming a theater actor, uses the app to connect with the volunteer from ShanghaiPRIDE to arrange an interview for its theatre program (Figure 5.7).

In the fourth episode of this miniseries, the lighthearted tone has a slight turn as one of the characters, Anda's mother, shows up after Anda refuses to go to a matchmaking arranged by her family. The mother scolds Anda, blames the "homosexual friends" who live nearby for having a bad influence on her, slams the door, and walks away. Yet this dramatic conflict of "coming out" is easily resolved when Anda shows her successful career achievements. Very quickly, the mother accepts Anda's sexuality. Anda seeks help from her apartment friend's mother who is affiliated with PFLAG China, an NGO that provides help to LGBT people to come out to their families and friends. *The L Bang* not only represents the "apartment plot"; it also exemplifies the "community plot" where the app itself functions as a narrative device that connects people across interior and exterior spaces. The video promotes the app and teaches viewers how the app is used; it also constructs a sense of community and visibility. Though the "light" entertainment, with a focus on young and urban middle-class lifestyle, has its limitations, the entrepreneurial aspiration of the app and everyday community concerns are not mutually exclusive. In episode 3, for example, all six characters, including five queer women and one gay man, gather in the apartment to help Muzi deal with her family pressure to date a man. Connected via the app The L (Rela), all the characters form the L Bang (where "bang" in Chinese is "gang"). At the same time, "bang" in Chinese means help, and the L Bang members are literally helping out each other. In this scene, when Muzi is contemplating the idea of entering an informal marriage with a gay man, the gang tries to introduce her to several potential gay men. Though the matchmaking is presented in a comedic tone, the process reveals the gender inequality between gay men and lesbian women, in which women are loaded with expectations to have children and perform the role of giving emotional support, even in a collaborative marriage with a gay man. Conducted in a lighthearted, if not sarcastic tone, the harsh reality makes Muzi drop the idea of marrying a gay man. This episode hence provides a helpful script to explore personal pressure in a community setting facilitated by the present-time connectivity and relationality among women.

Moreover, The L (Rela) was shut down for months right after it sponsored an event in 2017 in which a dozen parents tried to help their LGBT children find a partner at a public park in Shanghai.[61] The L recorded the quarrel between the parents of gay people and the majority of straight parents in the park. The video was uploaded online and became viral before it was taken down. Right after this incident, The L was ordered to

shut down based on technical-related reasons for seven months.⁶² In this
context, the "lightness" of the platform is made obvious again, as things
that reflect or trigger social conflicts may damage the very survival of
the platform. Given this context, it is important to recognize the efforts
made and the consequences of platform-initiated community practices,
which cannot be explained simply as a new kind of homonormativity.

Conclusion: The Temporality of "Platformativity"

In his essay "Platformativity: Media Studies, Area Studies," Thomas
Lamarre proposes the notion of platformativity to describe a kind of
activity via platforms as an alternative approach to the "region-platform"
relation.⁶³ In this conception, platformization of Chinese society is not
a self-contained phenomenon but an assemblage made up of different fragmentary media practices and networks. As the case of LESDO
and The L (Rela) indicate, platformativity is not only shifting configu-
rations of various platforms in diverse geosocial contexts, but also the
assemblage of different discourses, infrastructures, and practices that
are deeply ingrained with social relations of gender, sexuality, and
temporality.

The temporality of the platform and platformativity are more contingent than progressive. LESDO and The L are indicative of an emergent pink economy in China, which is simultaneously encouraged by
venture capital and censored and regulated by government policies on
the homosexual content. Female same-sex social networking apps complicate the understanding of "platform capitalism"⁶⁴ that links platform
economy liberalization to the decline of state intervention. Specifically,
in this chapter, I use the notion of "platform presentism" to theorize the
"lightness" of social networking app related videos, in their tone, form,
and organizing manner as a kind of digital masquerade. Platform presentism points to the presence or relevance of the platform in redefin-
ing media genres and creating "light" entertainment content that plays
around state media censorship on homosexuality. It also marks a shift to
lighthearted stories that introduce new ways of narrative registers, gender expressions, and audiovisual aesthetics. This departs from the previous representation of lesbianism as the mournful past. These "light"
entertainment, with the prioritization of young and urban middle-class

lifestyle, has its limitations. These limitations are well recognized in the liberal paradigm critique, as represented by the criticism of homonormativity. Lisa Duggan's concern about how gay culture is depoliticized and anchored in domesticity and consumption[65] can easily apply to the app videos in their emphasis on urban middle-class lifestyle, including the fascinations about same-sex marriage expressed in *X-Love*. However, at the same time, as illustrated by *The L Bang* and its community plot, the dating app functions as a central narrative device and visual trope to construct the urban apartment and outdoor space as spaces of female same-sex intimacy and sociality, as well as community collectiveness, rather than domesticity and individual privacy.

LGBT content is seen as highly risky after the shutting down of The L (Rela), and both apps have reduced their online video business and turned to livestreaming.[66] Livestreaming pushes the temporal logic of the platform to an extreme presentness. It maximizes the duration users spend on it since the accumulated data flow can be turned into profit. Gender and sexuality are also important in the understanding of livestreaming. The bodies of female hosts, or *nüzhubo*, are emphasized through the infrastructure of popular livestreaming sites and reiterated by performers in complex and complicated ways.[67] What is the politics of temporality of this new platform? The question of temporality in various media formations is worth investigating as the development of platforms unfolds.

The complex, if not contradictory, platform presentism exemplified by the social app videos should not be seen as simply an abbreviation of the universal "network time" and the drive of "acceleration." At the same time, neither should it be reduced into a model of "alternative" platform developments, or platforms with "Chinese characteristics." Rather, it echoes the critique of feminist science and technology studies, which reveals that the temporality of the platform itself cannot be dissociated from social markers such as gender and sexuality.

Coda

On March 9, 2018, the day after International Women's Day, the social media account @FeministVoices that I examined in detail in chapter 1 was shut down by Weibo. Seven days later, the activists staged a disco gathering in place of a tomb worshipping (Figure c.1).[1] In traditional funeral rituals, it is believed that the spirit of the deceased will visit the living on the seventh day after their death. As this book starts with an unconventional wedding, it makes sense to end it with a funeral that commemorates the shutdown of a Weibo account. Just like the wedding was not a conventional celebration of romantic love, the funeral disco was not simply about mourning the @FeministVoices account. By making fun of the difficulty, if not the absurdity, of censorship, and by being carefully recorded through photos and videos and circulated online, this action was another example of *digital masquerade*. In many ways, the funeral disco captures the heart of the digital masquerade idea that I discussed throughout the book.

The form of the masquerade is apparent in the event's full-body colorful costumes, masked faces, and lighthearted tone against the background of the urban ruins. The colorful clothes and guerrilla-style performance resonates with Pussy Riot and their masking tactics I discuss in chapter 1. As explained by the organizer, the rainbow colors of the different costumes stood for the colors that represent a symbol of support for LGBT issues.[2] At the back of the picture, a person is wearing a costume shaped like a vagina, a prop used in the *Vagina Monologues* performances. Like Pussy Riot, the Chinese feminists are masquerading as what Braidotti calls "anonymous militants" that strategically making "temporary identity claims."[3] The poster being held at the center of the picture has the profile image of the @FeministVoices account printed on it; the Chinese characters literally translate as "the voice of rights feminism." This funeral disco, therefore, shows the convergence of queer discourse (in the form of the rainbow colors), feminism (in the form of

Figure C.1. Feminist activists stage a funeral disco for the shutdown of the @Feminist-Voices Weibo account. Image courtesy of *Feminist Voices*.

the vagina costume), and rights (as stated at the center of the image) that I explore in detail in this book.

First, as the Chinese characters *nüquan* in the upper part of the poster suggest, the book traces the ascendance of what I call new rights feminism in China in the new millennium. In contrast to previous feminists, the new generation of activists self-identifies as rights feminist; the new activists are new subjects of rights. Symbolized by the coexisting rainbow outfit and vagina costume in the picture, the book examines the cross-fertilization of new rights feminism and LGBT activism, specifically the *lala* movement and the participation of lesbian and queer women. Analyzing how the *lala* movement predated and gave rise to the new rights feminism, this book makes visible the structural forces, such as heteropatriarchy, that continues to marginalize the queer perspective in Chinese feminisms. Both new rights feminism and LGBT activism appropriate international human rights frameworks and domestic legal norms to deepen the understanding of rights. The book thus challenges heterocentrism in the existing historiography of gender and feminism about China.

Echoing the humorous masquerading and colorful bodies of the funeral disco, throughout the book I have used the notion of digital masquerade to theorize the assemblage of digital technology and feminist,
queer, and rights activism. The tactic of masking in new rights feminist
media activism, including masked actions and the alteration of bodily
images online, is not only caused by state censorship but also shaped by
the affordances of social media platforms like Weibo. The tactical, flexible, and situational uses of rights by feminist and queer activists and
organizations can be seen as "performative," especially in media-centric
articulations of rights. Digital masquerade is also evident in a new wave
of independent and community-based digital films that contests the
"authentic" homosexual subjects that function as objects of knowledge
in mainstream media. These digital films intervene in the ongoing debate between biological determinist and social constructionist views of
homosexuality. Digital video-making itself becomes an act of coming
out through testimonial, confessional, or performative modes of sound-
image relationship. Digital video is a vital medium to work *through and
within* the process of identification and community formation, which
exemplifies the logic of entanglement in digital masquerade. Furthermore, the distribution of these digital videos is tied to the transnational
queer film festival network, of which APQFFA is an example. The masquerading of film festivals as *huodong*, or activity, is also a tactical mode
of queer organizing. Besides these independent films and film festivals,
more commercialized online video productions on lesbian dating apps
inspire female same-sex desires and intimacy, thus generating new understandings of sociality among women. This is true, on the one hand,
of how these videos epitomize present-time connectivity among women
and, on the other, of how they perpetuate the consumerist exclusivity
and normativity of the platforms. The "platform presentism" in these
social app videos shows the "lightness" in their tone, form, and organizing manner as a kind of digital masquerade. Therefore, digital masquerade captures the complex relationship between individuals/communities
and digital media that is simultaneously disruptive of and conditioned
by state censorship, technological affordances, and dominant social
codes.

Many of these acts of digital masquerade are marked by their creative lightness. That is not to say that these articulations are always

lighthearted or humorous. Instead, they come across multiple terrains of feeling, including the coexisting melancholic lesbian subjects and the presentism of mobile urban life explored in chapter 5, the diverse first-person audiovisual constructions examined in chapter 3, and the provocative, angry expressions calling out sexual abuse and harassment explored in chapter 1 and the more recent #MeToo movement.[4] Regardless of these differences, digital masquerade theorizes the creative and critical practices of feminism, queerness, and rights, and the co-constitutive role of digital technology. Like the funeral disco that took place only seven days after the closing of the Weibo account, digital masquerade can sometimes be swift, ephemeral, and playful. It involves guerrilla-like acts in the negotiation of daily life.

Through analyzing acts of digital masquerade, the book identifies a variety of digital media forms (e.g., digital filmmaking and distribution, social media, e-journals) as important arenas for feminist and queer articulations. These digital forms become vital media to work through and within the process of new rights feminism articulation, queer identification, and community formation. The book thus provides a culturally specific study of digital technology as assemblage and entanglement that echoes Kara Keeling's theorization of "Queer OS," a "scholarly political project" that explores the constitutive relationship between gender, sexuality, rights, and media and information technology.[5] These digital masquerades intervene in current discussions of "liberal paradigm critique" in feminism, queer studies, and rights studies. The existing critique of feminist and queer liberalism is valid when we consider the transnational circulation of queer rights in the Asia-Pacific region and the focus on urban, middle-class lifestyles in commercialized entertainment. Still, just like the framing of China as illiberal overlooks significant social changes brought about by feminist and LGBT activism, feminist and queer activism should not be reduced only to the criticism of homonationalism, heteronormativity, or the critique of universal human rights. Rather, digital masquerades enable us to see the complexity in practices such as the queering of weddings, new rights feminism, the tactical use of rights-related concepts, first-person filmic expressions, festival organizing, and more commercial forms of lesbian entertainment videos. Digital masquerade and its many acts and modes generate the understanding of feminist and queer activism beyond the simple binary of resistance and submission to existing social norms.

The shifting shapes of digital masquerade as assemblages of feminist, queer, and rights articulation and technological affordance question the understanding of activism in illiberal contexts as inevitably involving a certain degree of compromise and conformity, which overlooks significant social changes impacted by feminist and LGBT activism. Instead, the idea of digital masquerade provides a theoretical framework to look at feminist and queer activism as assemblages of practices, discourses, media affordance, and social regulations, which can be ambivalent to state, capital, or other dominant social orders. This ambivalent relationship plays out in how media affordance and censorship shapes rights feminist activism and rights articulation. It is also evident in how film festival networks are subjected to queer rights regimes, or how dating app videos may replicate the logic of homonormativity. While acknowledging these possible ambivalences, digital masquerade provides a framework for understanding feminist and queer activism beyond the binary of agency and conformity.

Throughout the book, I have pointed out how cultural expressions of queer sexuality, particularly female same-sex intimacy, have been systematically curtailed by the Chinese state and mainstream media. This regulation is at times also imposed on new rights feminist activism. This is evident in the social media censorship of feminist activism and the detention of the Feminist Five; the film, media, and Internet censorship of homosexuality that shape queer digital filmmaking and the later dating app videos; and the state restrictions and crackdown on rights-related NGOs, public events, film festival organizing, and even community participation of dating apps. The specificities of media regulation, censorship, and industry development set the boundaries of this book's research, which focuses mainly on feminist and queer media culture in mainland China. Yet transnational and trans-regional connections and exchanges are also crucial in these cultural phenomena in China. From the tactical use of international human rights frameworks in chapter 2 to the transnational network of Asia-Pacific queer film festivals in chapter 4, this book draws on approaches such as Sinophone queer studies and inter-Asia referencing to make visible the transnational politics of knowledge production and the complexity and multiplicity of Chinese-ness.

In parallel to the shutdown of @FeministVoices, ShanghaiPRIDE, originally scheduled to take place in the summer of 2020, was also canceled. Launched in 2009, ShanghaiPRIDE has played a significant role in building community culture, as explored in the formation of community video-making and exhibition practices in chapters 3 and 4. It was featured in dating app-sponsored video culture, one example being the *L Bang* series examined in chapter 5. In 2016, China passed a new law that imposed stricter rules on foreign NGOs to register and operate in the country, which has impacted non-profit groups involved in issues such as the environment, education, and rights.[6] This law created new challenges for many domestic rights-related NGOs as they often collaborate with foreign organizations. These legal changes, together with the tightening of media censorship, gives rise to what Lin Song calls "systematic homophobia," a kind of institutionalized as well as individual heterosexism and homophobia.[7] While the operation of homophobia has always been institutionalized, the intensified political and media censorship in the current historical conjuncture deserves further scholarly investigation in the future. Following these changes, some activists I interviewed or talked to during my fieldwork for this book have left China.[8] How their diasporic experience continues to shape the development of feminist and queer activism remains to be seen.

The space for new rights feminism and queer activism charted in this book is declining, even though media-based feminist actions such as the #MeToo movement continue to flourish after 2018.[9] Paradoxically, at the same time, the term rights feminism has been popularized in unprecedented ways. For example, a popular forum website called Nüquan Ba, hosted by the web service giant Baidu, aims to provide a platform for users to discuss issues related to "women's status and rights and interests" (*nüxing diwei yu quanyi*). This forum has accumulated more than 1,400,000 posts to date.[10] These popularized discussions of feminisms on the Internet have taken the place of the new rights feminism examined in this book, and the meaning of the term *nüquan* has changed. Apart from the many meanings of rights I explored in this book, the connotation of feminism as female privilege was also developed in the context of gender antagonism mixed with class friction.[11] As mentioned in chapter 1, online misogyny has surfaced to respond to the rise of new rights feminism. The unprecedented visibility of rights feminism in mainstream online forums and the misogynistic backlash have pushed gender rivalry to another scale. The highly emotionally charged opposition between the genders displaces social anxiety concerning increasing economic inequality and class differences. In this context, the shifting meanings of contemporary Chinese feminisms as well as *quan* deserve further investigation in the future.

Against this backdrop of the mainstreaming of popular feminist discourses, this book contributes to the writing of the feminist and queer histories, some of which are more minor, mundane, and ephemeral. Perhaps writing this book is itself an act of queer masquerade, as it provides snapshots of the creative, rapidly-evolving development of new rights feminist and queer activism instead of a comprehensive history of contemporary feminist and queer politics. Ending this book with the funeral disco is just right: a funeral disco and the online circulation of this action represent the resurrection of the "dead" social media account. Despite the many obstacles to feminist, queer, and other forms of organizing, digital masquerades always assemble and emerge in unexpected, sometimes spectral ways.

ACKNOWLEDGMENTS

I could never have completed this book without the generous sharing of feminists and queer activists whom I have encountered since starting to research this project in 2014. Their creativity and resilience inspired me to write this book. I am grateful to those who shared their thoughts with me and offered help along the way. My heartfelt appreciation also goes to the artists and activists who gave me the permission to use their images in this book.

Writing this book has been a long journey. I am deeply grateful to have Rey Chow, Petrus Liu, and Lisa Rofel along the way. They have kindly given me academic feedback at different stages. I am also grateful to Helen Leung and Christine Kim for inviting me to present a part of this book in the Inter-Asia Beyond Asia workshop at Simon Fraser University. My thanks also go to Margaret Hillenbrand, who invited me to present my research at Oxford University. I am indebted to Chris Berry, Audrey Yue, Jeroen de Kloet, and Yomi Braester for their guidance.

Looking back, many people have paved my path in the academia. My special thanks go to Dai Jinhua in Peking University, whose classes inspired me to pursue a career in film and media research. I am indebted to David E. James, Akira Lippit, and Priya Jaikumar, who expanded my intellectual horizons. Kara Keeling has always been a source of inspiration. I have benefited enormously from my conversations with her. Marsha Kinder, Ellen Seiter, Michael Renov, Tara McPherson, and Aniko Imre have shown me how to be a successful scholar and a dedicated teacher. I am grateful for their generosity, support, and friendship. My dearest and fondest memory belongs to Anne Friedberg, with whom I had the pleasure to work during my defining years at the School of Cinematic Arts at the University of Southern California. I also want to thank Philip Rosen, Stanley Rosen, Meiling Cheng, Mary Ann Doane, Wendy Chun, Lynne Joyrich, Gaylyn Studlar, Matthew Johnson, Zhang

Zhen, Adrienne Shaw, Katherine Sender, and Angelina Chin for their encouragement and support.

I am blessed with a vibrant intellectual community while writing this book in Hong Kong. My colleagues at the Division of Cultural Studies at the Chinese University of Hong Kong have been generous and supportive. I am grateful to Song Hwee Lim and Laikwan Pang for their guidance, support, and comments on my project. I am fortunate to have support from my colleagues Katrien Jacobs, Kaming Wu, Peichi Chung, Rolien Hoyng, Murat Es, Elmo Gonzaga, Benny Lim, Tiecheng Li, and Janet Pang. As a founding member of the Hong Kong Scholars Alliance for Sexual and Gender Diversity, I am fortunate to work with scholars across different universities in Hong Kong. I am grateful to the friendship and support from Lucetta Kam, Day Wong, Travis Kong, Yiu-fai Chow, Kit Hung, Franco Lai, Sealing Cheng, Alvin Wong, and Siu Cho. My appreciation also goes to Bo Zheng, John Erni, Anthony Fung, Emilie Yeh, Shengqing Wu, Stephen Chu, Diana Lemberg, Denise Tang, Lik Sam Chan, and Kenny Ng.

Without the funding by two external grants from the Research Grants Council operated under the University Grants Committee in Hong Kong, including an Early Career Scheme Grant (number 22607115) and General Research Fund (number 14612818), this book project would not have been completed. This book also receives support from Direct Grant for Research (number 4051095), and the Publication Subvention Fund from the Faculty of Arts at the Chinese University of Hong Kong. My special thanks is given to Xiaobing Tang, Dean of the Faculty of Arts, for his encouragement and support. Aside from the substantial funding, many people assisted me with different parts of the book: Darren Fung, Zabrina Lo, and Lixian Hou, who gathered, translated, and edited research materials; my postgraduate students Yiming Wang, Zongyi Zhang, and Chengjie Xiao, who helped me in various ways.

Conversations with people at the International Communication Association Conference in Washington, D.C., the Crossroads in Cultural Studies Conference in Shanghai and Sydney, the Inter-Asia Conferences in Seoul and Surabaya, and the Visible Evidence conference in New Delhi were immensely helpful for my book writing process.

The editorial team at New York University Press has been devoted and encouraging to this project from the beginning. I am indebted to Karen

Tongson for the encouragement and faith in my project, Eric Zinner and Henry Jenkins for their expertise and patience, and Furqan Sayeed and Ainee Jeong for their professional and kind help. I am enormously grateful to the two anonymous reviewers who offered crucial feedback and constructive suggestions.

There are no words to describing my gratitude to Yin Wang, Feng-mei Herbert, Fiona Ng, Qi Wang, and Chun-yen Wang for their support and friendship. I am blessed to have a group of excellent colleagues and friends whom I knew from the University of Southern California; among them are Chunchi Wang, Stephanie Debore, Kristy Kang, Hyung-sook Lee, Dong Hoon Kim, Casey Riffel, Chera Kee, Annie Manion, Gloria Kim, Adán Avalos, Nam Lee, and HyeRyoung Ok. I am also grateful to the warm support of Kick Li, Dian Dian, Hui Zhang, Jiayun Zhuang, Fangc-hun Li, Chaohua Wang, Yurou Zhong, Yu-fang Cho, Yiman Wang, Calvin Hui, Tan Hoang Nguyen, Dredge Kang, Yifei Eric Wu, Peng Tu, Ian Chen, and Jing Guo, who make this journey unforgettable. Last but not least, I am fortunate to have Oi-lam Ng and her love, support, and unfailing belief in me.

NOTES

INTRODUCTION. DIGITAL MASQUERADE

1 Maizi Li, "When She Is Married to Her, the Background of *Tongzhi* Wedding in China," NGOCN, August 20, 2015, http://ngocn.blog.caixin.com.

2 Li, "When She Is Married to Her."

3 Dune Lawrence and David Ramli, "A Chinese Dating App for Gay Men Is Helping Them Have Kids, Too," *Bloomberg Businessweek*, March 21, 2019, www.bloomberg .com.

4 Catherine Shu, "Alibaba's Latest Marketing Campaign Supports Same-Sex Marriage," TechCrunch, accessed March 5, 2018, https://techcrunch.com.

5 Lisa Duggan, *The Twilight of Equality? Neoliberalism, Cultural Politics, and the Attack on Democracy* (Boston: Beacon Press, 2003).

6 Jasbir K. Puar, *Terrorist Assemblages: Homonationalism in Queer Times* (Durham, NC: Duke University Press, 2007).

7 Tingting Wei, "The Same-Sex Wedding I Hosted," GDotTV, July 12, 2015, http://gdottv.com.

8 See Xiaopei He, "My Unconventional Marriage or Ménage à Trois in Beijing," in *As Normal as Possible: Negotiating Sexuality and Gender in Mainland China and Hong Kong*, ed. Yau Ching (Hong Kong: Hong Kong University Press), 103–10.

9 For more information on this event, see Tania Branigan, "Beijing's 'Happy Couples' Launch Campaign for Same-Sex Marriages," Guardian, February 24, 2009, www.theguardian.com.

10 Leta Hong Fincher, *Betraying the Big Brother: The Feminist Awakening in China* (New York: Verso Books, 2021).

11 I use terms such as LGBT or *ku'er* as they are referred by the activists in specific contexts. Compared to LGBTQ+, LGBT is more commonly used. In a more general sense, I may use LGBT and queer interchangeably to refer to non-normative sexuality in this book.

12 For the history of how queer people appropriate the term *tongzhi* in Taiwan and Hong Kong, see Song Hwee Lim, "How to Be Queer in Taiwan: Translation, Appropriation, and the Construction of a Queer Identity in Taiwan" in *AsiaPacifiQueer: Rethinking Genders and Sexualities*, ed. Fran Martin, Peter A. Jackson, Mark McLelland, and Audrey Yue (Champaign: University of Illinois Press, 2008): 235–50. For the development in mainland China, see Hongwei Bao, *Queer Comrades: Gay Identity and Tongzhi Activism in Postsocialist China* (Copenhagen: NIAS Press, 2018).

13 Nancy Fraser, "Feminism, Capitalism and the Cunning of History," *New Left Review* 56 (March–April 2009): 108.

14 David L. Eng, *The Feeling of Kinship: Queer Liberalism and the Racialization of Intimacy* (Durham, NC: Duke University Press, 2010).

15 Jacques Rancière, "Who Is the Subject of the Rights of Man?" *South Atlantic Quarterly* 103, no. 2–3 (2004): 297–310.

16 John Nguyet Erni, "Cultural Studies Meets Rights Criticism," *Communication and Critical/Cultural Studies* 10, no. 2–3 (2013): 238–41; Lydia H. Liu, "Shadows of Universalism: The Untold Story of Human Rights around 1948," *Critical Inquiry* 40, no. 4 (2014): 385–417.

17 Robin Blackburn, "Reclaiming Human Rights," *New Left Review*, no. 69 (May–June 2010): 136.

18 Inderpal Grewal, "'Women's Rights as Human Rights': Feminist Practices, Global Feminism, and Human Rights Regimes in Transnationality," *Citizenship Studies* 3, no. 3 (1999): 337–54.

19 Grewal, "Women's Rights."

20 Sealing Cheng, "The Paradox of Vernacularization: Women's Human Rights and the Gendering of Nationhood," *Anthropological Quarterly* 84, no. 2 (Spring 2011): 475–505.

21 Lisa Yoneyama, *Cold War Ruins: Transpacific Critique of American Justice and Japanese War Crimes* (Durham, NC: Duke University Press, 2016).

22 Adetoun O. Ilumoka, "African Women's Economic, Social and Cultural Rights: Towards a Relevant Theory and Practice," in *Human Rights of Women: National and International Perspectives*, ed. Rebecca J. Cook (Philadelphia: University of Pennsylvania Press, 1994), 307–25.

23 Julietta Hua, *Trafficking Women's Human Rights* (Minneapolis: University of Minnesota Press, 2011).

24 Lisa Duggan, "The New Homonormativity: The Sexual Politics of Neoliberalism," in *Materializing Democracy: Toward a Revitalized Cultural Politics*, ed. Russ Castronovo and Dana D. Nelson (Durham, NC: Duke University Press, 2002), 175–94; Jasbir K. Puar, *Terrorist Assemblages: Homonationalism in Queer Times* (Durham, NC: Duke University Press, 2007).

25 Arnaldo Cruz-Malave and Martin F. Manalansan IV, "Introduction: Dissident Sexualities/Alternative Globalisms," in *Queer Globalizations: Citizenship and the Afterlife of Colonialism*, ed. Arnaldo Cruz-Malave and Martin F. Manalansan IV (New York: New York University Press, 2002), 6.

26 Aili Mari Tripp, "The Evolution of Transnational Feminisms: Consensus, Conflict, and New Dynamics," in *Global Feminism: Transnational Women's Activism, Organizing, and Human Rights*, ed. Myra Marx Ferree and Aili Mari Tripp (New York: New York University Press, 2006), 51–75.

27 Tripp, "The Evolution of Transnational Feminisms," 65.

28 Omar G. Encarnacion, "International Influence, Domestic Activism, and Gay Rights in Argentina," *Political Science Quarterly* 128, no. 4 (Winter 2013): 698.

29 Lynette J. Chua, "The Vernacular Mobilization of Human Rights in Myanmar's Sexual Orientation and Gender Identity Movement," *Law & Society Review* 49, no. 2 (2015): 299–332.

30 Chua, "Vernacular Mobilization."

31 Arzoo Osanloo, *The Politics of Women's Rights in Iran* (Princeton, NJ: Princeton University Press, 2009).

32 Marina Svensson, *Debating Human Rights in China: A Conceptual and Political History* (Lanham, MD: Rowman & Littlefield Publishers, 2002).

33 Mizuyo Sudo, "Concepts of Women's Rights in Modern China," trans. Michael G. Hill, *Gender & History* 18, no. 3 (2006): 472–89.

34 Sudo, "Concepts of Women's Rights in Modern China," 480.

35 Sudo, "Concepts of Women's Rights in Modern China," 480.

36 Zheng Wang, *Women in the Chinese Enlightenment: Oral and Textual Histories* (Berkeley: University of California Press, 1999).

37 The term *nüxing zhuyi* was widely used in academic studies, especially literary and cultural studies. Representative works include the publication of a book series entitled Feminism in China (*zhongguo nüxing zhuyi*), edited by Huang Lin. The first book was published in 2004. Up to 2011, the series has published twelve volumes.

38 Lisa Rofel, "Grassroots Activism: Non-Normative Sexual Politics in Post-Socialist China" in *Unequal China: The Political Economy and Cultural Politics of Inequality*, ed. Wanning Sun and Yingjie Guo (New York: Routledge, 2013), 154–67.

39 Jian Chang, ed., *The Securing of Human Rights in Contemporary China* (Beijing: Zhongguo Renmin Daxue Chubanshe, 2015); Chunde Gu, *Studies on the Theory and Practice of Human Rights with Chinese Characteristics* (Beijing: Zhongguo Renmin Daxue Chubanshe, 2013).

40 Ching Kwan Lee, "Rights Activism in China," *Contexts* 7, no. 3 (2008): 14–19.

41 Elizabeth J. Perry, "Chinese Conceptions of 'Rights': From Mencius to Mao—and Now," *Perspectives on Politics* 6, no. 1 (2008): 37–50.

42 Ching Kwan Lee and You-tien Hsing, "Social Activism in China: Agency and Possibility," in *Reclaiming Chinese Society: The New Social Activism*, ed. You-tien Hsing and Ching Kwan Lee (Abingdon, UK: Routledge, 2010), 1–13.

43 For the history of the discussion on queerness and the use of the term *ku'er*, see Jia Tan, "Beijing Meets Hawai'i: Reflections on Ku'er, Indigeneity, and Queer Theory," *GLQ: A Journal of Lesbian and Gay Studies* 23, no. 1 (2017): 137–50.

44 Lisa Rofel, *Desiring China: Experiments in Neoliberalism, Sexuality, and Public Culture* (Durham, NC: Duke University Press, 2007).

45 Travis S. K. Kong, *Chinese Male Homosexualities: Memba, Tongzhi and Golden Boy* (London and New York: Routledge, 2011): 203.

46 Petrus Liu, *Queer Marxism in Two Chinas* (Durham, NC: Duke University Press, 2015), 7.

47 Liu, *Queer Marxism in Two Chinas*, 10.

48 Liu, *Queer Marxism in Two Chinas*, 7.

49 Audrey Yue, "Queer Singapore: An Introduction," in *Queer Singapore: Illiberal Citizenship and Mediated Cultures*, edited by Audrey Yue and Jun Zubillaga-Pow (Hong Kong: Hong Kong University Press, 2012).

50 "Masquerade," Oxford English Dictionary, www.oed.com.

51 Joan Riviere, "Womanliness as a Masquerade," *International Journal of Psychoanalysis* 10 (1929): 1–5.

52 Riviere, "Womanliness as a Masquerade."

53 Laura Mulvey, "Afterthoughts on 'Visual Pleasure and Narrative Cinema' Inspired by 'Duel in the Sun,'" *Framework* 15/16/17 (Summer 1981): 12–15.

54 Mary Ann Doane, "Film and the Masquerade: Theorising the Female Spectator," *Screen* 23, no. 3–4 (1982): 74–88.

55 Chris Straayer, *Deviant Eyes, Deviant Bodies: Sexual Re-orientations in Film and Video* (New York: Columbia University Press, 1996).

56 Straayer, 141.

57 Straayer, 141.

58 Straayer, 141.

59 Kathleen Woodward, "Youthfulness as a Masquerade," *Discourse* 11, no. 1 (Fall–Winter 1988): 125.

60 Ellen Jean Samuels, "My Body, My Closet: Invisible Disability and the Limits of Coming-out Discourse," *GLQ: A Journal of Lesbian and Gay Studies* 9, no. 1 (2003): 240.

61 Jack Halberstam, *Female Masculinity* (Durham, NC: Duke University Press, 2019), 20.

62 Judith Butler, *Gender Trouble: Feminism and the Subversion of Identity* (New York: Routledge, 2006), 187.

63 Halberstam, *Female Masculinity*.

64 Tobin Siebers, *Disability Theory* (Ann Arbor: University of Michigan Press, 2008), 116.

65 Samuels, 240.

66 Samuels, 244.

67 Mykel Johnson, "Butchy Femme," in *Persistent Desire*, ed. Joan Nestle (Boston: Alyson Publication, 1992), 397–98.

68 Siebers, "Disability as Masquerade," in *Disability Theory* (University of Michigan Press, 2008), 103.

69 Siebers, 103.

70 Siebers, 100.

71 Jing Wang, *The Other Digital China: Nonconfrontational Activism on the Social Web* (Cambridge, MA: Harvard University Press, 2019).

72 Wang, *The Other Digital China*, 42.

73 Elisabeth L. Engebretsen, "Of Pride and Visibility: The Contingent Politics of Queer Grassroots Activism in China," in *Queer/Tongzhi China: New Perspectives on Research, Activism and Media Cultures*, ed. Elisabeth L. Engebretsen and William F. Schroeder (Copenhagen: NIAS Press, 2015), 95.

74 Yue, "Queer Singapore."

75 Jay David Bolter and Richard Grusin, *Remediation: Understanding New Media* (Cambridge, MA: MIT Press, 2000); Lev Manovich, *The Language of New Media* (Cambridge, MA: MIT Press, 2001); Stephen Wilson, *Information Arts: Intersections of Art, Science, and Technology* (Cambridge, MA: MIT Press, 2003).

76 Wendy Hui Kyong Chun, "Introduction: Race and/as Technology; or, How to Do Things to Race," *Camera Obscura* 24, no. 1 (May 20, 2009): 7–35; Nina B. Huntemann and Ben Aslinger, eds., *Gaming Globally: Production, Play, and Place* (New York: Palgrave Macmillan, 2013); Lisa Nakamura, *Digitizing Race: Visual Cultures of the Internet* (Minneapolis: University of Minnesota Press, 2007).

77 Judy Wajcman, *Pressed for Time: The Acceleration of Life in Digital Capitalism* (Chicago: University of Chicago Press, 2015).

78 Wajcman, *Pressed for Time*, 35.

79 Jennifer Daryl Slack and J. Macgregor Wise, *Culture and Technology: A Primer* (New York: Peter Lang, 2005), 111.

80 Slack and Wise, 111.

81 Slack and Wise, 132.

82 Gilles Deleuze and Félix Guattari, *A Thousand Plateaus: Capitalism and Schizophrenia*, trans. Brian Massumi (Minneapolis: University of Minnesota Press, 1987), 90, quoted in Slack and Wise, 133.

83 Elizabeth Grosz, *Architecture from the Outside: Essays on Virtual and Real Space* (Cambridge, Massachusetts: MIT Press, 2001), 182.

84 Cara Wallis, *Technomobility in China: Young Migrant Women and Mobile Phones* (New York: New York University Press, 2013), 6.

85 Wallis, *Technomobility in China*, 6.

86 Wallis, *Technomobility in China*, 3.

87 Wallis, *Technomobility in China*, 7.

88 Wallis, *Technomobility in China*, 185.

89 Wallis, *Technomobility in China*, 185.

90 Karen Barad, *Meeting the Universe Halfway: Quantum Physics and the Entanglement of Matter and Meaning* (Durham, NC: Duke University Press, 2007).

91 Anne Balsamo, *Designing Culture: The Technological Imagination at Work* (Durham, NC: Duke University Press, 2011), 37.

92 Karen Barad, "Posthumanist Performativity: Toward an Understanding of How Matter Comes to Matter," *Signs* 28, no. 3 (2003): 801–31.

93 Barad, *Meeting the Universe Halfway*, ix.

94 Sara Ahmed, "Open Forum Imaginary Prohibitions: Some Preliminary Remarks on the Founding Gestures of the 'New Materialism,'" *European Journal of Women's Studies* 15, no. 1 (2008): 33.

95 Rey Chow, *Entanglements, or Transmedial Thinking about Capture* (Durham, NC: Duke University Press, 2012), 11.

96 Y. Lê Espiritu, L. Lowe, and L. Yoneyama, "Transpacific Entanglements," in *Flashpoints for Asian American Studies* (New York: Fordham University Press, 2017), 175–89.

97 John Edward Campbell, *Getting It on Online: Cyberspace, Gay Male Sexuality, and Embodied Identity* (New York: Harrington Park Press, 2004); Eve Ng, "A 'Post-Gay' Era? Media Gaystreaming, Homonormativity, and the Politics of LGBT Integration," *Communication, Culture & Critique* 6, no. 2 (June 10, 2013): 258–83; Eve Ng and Sophie Toupin, "Feminist and Queer Practices in the Online and Offline Activism of Occupy Wall Street," *Networking Knowledge* 6, no. 3 (2013): 90–114; Sonia Nuñez Puente, "Feminist Cyberactivism: Violence against Women, Internet Politics, and Spanish Feminist Praxis Online," *Continuum* 25, no. 3 (2011): 333–46; Sonia Núñez Puente and Antonio García Jiménez, "New Technologies and New Spaces for Relation: Spanish Feminist Praxis Online," *European Journal of Women's Studies* 16, no. 3 (2009): 249–63; Kate O'Riordan, and David J. Philips, *Queer Online: Media Technology & Sexuality* (New York: Peter Lang, 2007).

98 Chris Berry, Fran Martin, and Audrey Yue, eds., *Mobile Cultures: New Media in Queer Asia* (Durham, NC: Duke University Press, 2003); Peter A. Jackson, "Capitalism, LGBT Activism, and Queer Autonomy in Thailand," in *Queer Bangkok: 21st Century Markets, Media, and Rights*, ed. Peter A. Jackson (Hong Kong: Hong Kong University Press, 2011), 195–204; Elisabeth L. Engebretsen, William F. Schroeder, and Hongwei Bao, eds., *Queer/Tongzhi China: New Perspectives on Research, Activism and Media Cultures* (Copehagen: Nias Press, 2014); for the construction of Asian-ness in a transnational context, see Tan Hoang Nguyen, *A View from the Bottom: Asian American Masculinity and Sexual Representation* (Durham, NC: Duke University Press, 2014).

99 Kara Keeling, "Queer OS," *Cinema Journal* 53, no. 2 (2014): 153.

100 Keeling, "Queer OS," 153.

101 Xueqing Li, Francis L. F. Lee, and Ying Li, "The Dual Impact of Social Media under Networked Authoritarianism: Social Media Use, Civic Attitudes, and System Support in China," *International Journal of Communication* 10 (2016): 5143–63; Rebecca MacKinnon, "Liberation Technology: China's 'Networked Authoritarianism,'" *Journal of Democracy* 22, no. 2 (2011): 32–46.

102 Simon Shen and Shaun Breslin, eds., *Online Chinese Nationalism and China's Bilateral Relations, Online Chinese Nationalism and China's Bilateral Relations* (Lanham, MD: Lexington Books, 2010); Xu Wu, *Chinese Cyber Nationalism: Evolution, Characteristics, and Implications* (Lanham, MD: Lexington Books, 2007); Guobin Yang, *The Power of the Internet in China: Citizen Activism Online* (New York: Columbia University Press, 2009).

103 Gang Chen and Jinjing Zhu, "Behind the 'Green Dam': Internet Censorship in China" (Singapore: East Asian Institute, National University of Singapore, 2009); Eric Harwit and Duncan Clark, "Shaping the Internet in China: Evolution of Political Control over Network Infrastructure and Content," *Asian Survey* 41, no. 3 (2001): 377–408; Daniela Stockmann and Mary E. Gallagher, "Remote Control: How the Media Sustain Authoritarian Rule in China," *Comparative Political Studies* 44, no. 4 (2011).

104 Jack Linchuan Qiu, *Working-Class Network Society: Communication Technology and the Information Have-Less in Urban China* (Cambridge, MA: MIT Press, 2009); Yang, *Power*; Guobin Yang, "Internet Activism & the Party-State in China," *Dædalus* 143, no. 2 (2014): 110–23.
105 Guobin Yang, *The Power of the Internet in China: Citizen Activism Online* (New York: Columbia University Press, 2009); Guobin Yang, "Internet Activism & the Party-State in China," *Daedalus* 143, no. 2 (2014): 110–23.
106 Hamid Naficy, *An Accented Cinema: Exilic and Diasporic Filmmaking* (Princeton, NJ: Princeton University Press, 2001).

1. DIGITAL MASKING AND MASQUERADE

An earlier version of parts of chapter 1 has appeared in Jia Tan, "Digital Masquerading: Feminist Media Activism in China" in *Crime, Media, Culture* 13, no. 2 (2017): 171–86.
1 Jing Xiong, personal communication, February 26, 2016.
2 Anonymous, personal communication, June 14, 2019.
3 Anonymous, personal communication, November 21, 2021.
4 For more details on anti-Muslim sentiments on Chinese social media, see Luwei Rose Luqiu and Fan Yang, "Anti-Muslim Sentiment on Social Media in China and Chinese Muslims' Reactions to Hatred and Misunderstanding," *Chinese Journal of Communication* 13, no. 3 (2020): 258–74.
5 Anonymous, personal communication, November 21, 2021.
6 Andrew Jacobs, "Taking Feminist Battle to China's Streets, and Landing in Jail," *New York Times*, April 5, 2015, accessed June 20, 2016, www.nytimes.com.
7 Gary King, Jennifer Pan, and Margaret E. Roberts, "How Censorship in China Allows Government Criticism but Silences Collective Expression," *American Political Science Review* 107, no. 2 (May 2013): 326–43.
8 David Morley, *Family Television: Cultural Power and Domestic Leisure* (London: Routledge, 1986); Janice A. Radway, *Reading the Romance: Women, Patriarchy and Popular Literature* (Chapel Hill: University of North Carolina Press, 1984).
9 Henry Jenkins, *Textual Poachers: Television Fans and Participatory Culture* (London and New York: Routledge, 1992); Henry Jenkins, *Convergence Culture: Where Old and New Media Collide* (New York: New York University Press, 2006).
10 Wilma de Jong, Martin Shaw, and Neil Stammers, *Global Activism, Global Media* (London: Pluto Press, 2005); Joss Hands, *@ is for Activism: Dissent, Resistance and Rebellion in a Digital Culture* (London: Pluto Press, 2011); Meg McLagan, "Spectacles of Difference: Cultural Activism and the Mass Mediation," in *Media Worlds: Anthropology on New Terrain, Berkeley, Los Angeles*, ed. Faye D. Ginsburg, Lila Abu-Lughod, and Brian Larkin (London: University of California Press, 2002), 90–111; John D. H. Downing, *Radical Media: Rebellious Communication and Social Movements* (Thousand Oaks, CA: Sage Publications, 2001); Chris Greer and Eugene McLaughlin, "We Predict a Riot? Public Order Policing, New Media

Environments and the Rise of the Citizen Journalist," *British Journal of Criminology* 50, no. 6 (July 2010): 1041–59.

11 Manuel Castells, *Networks of Outrage and Hope: Social Movements in the Internet Age* (Cambridge: Polity Press, 2012); Bernard Stiegler, *Acting Out* (Stanford, CA: Stanford University Press, 2008).

12 Natalie Fenton and Veronica Barassi, "Alternative Media and Social Networking Sites: The Politics of Individuation and Political Participation," *Communication Review* 14, no. 3 (September 2011):179–96; Tiziana Terranova, *Network Culture: Politics for the Information Age* (London: Pluto, 2004).

13 King-wa Fu, Chung-hong Chan, and Michael Chau, "Assessing censorship on microblogs in China: Discriminatory keyword analysis and the real-name registration policy," *IEEE Internet Computing* 17, no. 3 (2013): 42-50.

14 Gary King, Jennifer Pan, and Margaret E. Roberts, "How Censorship in China Allows Government Criticism but Silences Collective Expression," *American Political Science Review* (2013): 326–43.

15 Gillian Bolsover and Philip Howard, "Chinese Computational Propaganda: Automation, Algorithms and the Manipulation of Information about Chinese Politics on Twitter and Weibo," *Information, Communication & Society* 22, no. 14 (2019): 2063–80.

16 Jonathan Hassid, "The Politics of China's Emerging Micro-Blogs: Something New or More of the Same?" (APSA 2012 Annual Meeting Paper, New Orleans, LA, July 14, 2012), 1–25.

17 Cao Yin, "Police Urged to Boost Use of Micro Blogs," *China Daily*, September 27, 2011, accessed January 21, 2016, www.chinadailyasia.com; Hassid, "The Politics of China's," 1–25.

18 Guobin Yang, "Internet Activism & the Party-State in China," *Daedalus* 143, no. 2 (April 2014): 110–23.

19 Guobin Yang, "Contesting Food Safety in the Chinese Media: Between Hegemony and Counter-Hegemony," *China Quarterly* 214 (June 2013): 337–55.

20 Yangqi Tong and Shaohua Lei, "War of Position and Microblogging in China," *Journal of Contemporary China* 22, no. 80 (November 2013): 292–311.

21 Xiao Qiang, "The Battle for the Chinese Internet," *Journal of Democracy* 22, no. 2 (April 2011): 47–61.

22 Rebecca A. Clothey et al., "A Voice for the Voiceless: Online Social Activism in Uyghur Language Blogs and State Control of the Internet in China," *Information, Communication & Society* 19, no. 6 (July 2015): 858–74.

23 Cara Wallis, "Gender and China's Online Censorship Protest Culture," *Feminist Media Studies* 15, no. 2 (2015): 223–38.

24 Jun Li and Xiaoqin Li, "Media as a Core Political Resource: The Young Feminist Movements in China," *Chinese Journal of Communication* 10, no. 1 (2017): 54–71.

25 Bin Wang and Catherine Driscoll, "Chinese Feminists on Social Media: Articulating Different Voices, Building Strategic Alliances," *Continuum* 33, no. 1 (2019): 1–15.

26 Lixian Hou, "Rewriting 'the Personal Is Political': Young Women's Digital Activism and New Feminist Politics in China," *Inter-Asia Cultural Studies* 21, no. 3 (2020): 337–55.

27 Harriet Evans, "Sexed Bodies, Sexualized Identities, and the Limits of Gender," *China Information* 22, no. 2 (July 2008): 361–86; Christina K. Gilmartin et al., eds., *Engendering China: Women, Culture, and the State* (Cambridge, MA: Harvard University Press, 1994).

28 Lisa Rofel, *Desiring China: Experiments in Neoliberalism, Sexuality, and Public Culture* (Durham, NC: Duke University Press, 2007).

29 Evans, "Sexed Bodies," 361–86.

30 Jun Zhang and Peidong Sun, "'When Are You Going to Get Married?' Parental Matchmaking and Middle-Class Women in Contemporary Urban China," in *Wives, Husbands, and Lovers: Marriage and Sexuality in Hong Kong, Taiwan, and Urban China*, ed. Deborah Davis and Sara Friedman (Stanford: Stanford University Press, 2014), 118–44.

31 Cecilia Milwertz and Wei Bu, "Non-Governmental Feminist Activism in The People's Republic of China: Communicating Oppositional Gender Equality Knowledge," in *Social Movements in China and Hong Kong: The Expansion of Protest Space*, ed. Gilles Guiheux and Khun Eng Kuah-Pearce (Amsterdam: Amsterdam University Press, 2009), 227–44.

32 Milwertz and Bu, "Non-Governmental Feminist Activism," 228.

33 Milwertz and Bu, "Non-Governmental Feminist Activism," 227–44.

34 Ping-Chun Hsiung and Yuk-Lin Renita Wong, "Jie Gui—Connecting the Tracks: Chinese Women's Activism Surrounding the 1995 World Conference on Women in Beijing," *Gender & History* 10, no. 3 (November 1998): 480.

35 Ping-Chun Hsiung, Maria Jaschok, and Cecilia Milwertz, eds., *Chinese Women Organizing: Cadres, Feminists, Muslims, Queers* (Oxford: Berg, 2001).

36 Wei Bu and Zhang Qi, eds., *Xiaochu jiating baoli yu meijie changdao: yanjiu, jianzheng yu shijian* [Media Activism to End Domestic Violence: Research, Witness Reports, and Practice] (Beijing: Zhongguo Shehui Kexue Chubanshe, 2011).

37 Wei Bu, "Girls' Issues, Gender and the Media: Feminist Activisms in China," in *The International Handbook of Children, Media and Culture*, ed. Kirsten Drotner and Sonia Livingstone (Los Angeles: Sage, 2008), 314–26.

38 Chris Berry, Lu Xinyu, and Lisa Rofel, *The New Chinese Documentary Movement: For the Public Record* (Hong Kong: Hong Kong University Press, 2010).

39 For a detailed analysis of Ai's works, see Zeng Jinyan, *Feminism and Genesis of the Citizen Intelligentsia in China* (Hong Kong: City University of Hong Kong Press, 2016).

40 Zhang Zhen, "Toward a Digital Political Mimesis: Aesthetic of Affect and Activist Video," in *DV-Made China: Digital Subjects and Social Transformations after Independent Film*, ed. Zhang Zhen and Angela Zito (Honolulu: University of Hawai'i Press, 2015), 335.

41 Zhang, "Toward a Digital Political Mimesis," 332–54.

42 Zhang, "Toward a Digital Political Mimesis," 332–54.

43 Zhang, "Toward a Digital Political Mimesis," 352.

44 Jun Li, personal communication, January 10, 2016.

45 Lü Pin, "Zheng qu zhu liu yu bao chi ling lei [Strive for Mainstream and Keep the Alternative]," *Nandu*, accessed June 20, 2016, www.nandu.com.

46 Bu, "Girls' Issues, Gender and the Media," 322.

47 @FeministVoices (*nüquan zhi sheng*) is associated with the Beijing Gender Culture Communication Center, Media Monitor for Women Network in Beijing, an organization that promotes gender equality in the media and women's communication rights through research, training, advocacy, writing, and media liaison. @WomenAwakening (*xin meiti nüxing*) is based in Guangzhou.

48 Shu-mei Shih, "Towards an Ethics of Transnational Encounters, or 'When' Does a 'Chinese' Woman Become a 'Feminist'?" In *Dialogue and Difference* (New York: Palgrave Macmillan, 2005), 3–28.

49 Dongchao Min, *Translation and Travelling Theory: Feminist Theory and Praxis in China* (London and New York: Routledge, 2017), 42.

50 For a detailed discussion of the process of translating feminism, see Min, *Translation and Travelling Theory*, 45–49.

51 Wen Liu, Ana Huang, and Jingchao Ma, "Young Activists, New Movements: Contemporary Chinese Queer Feminism and Transnational Genealogies," *Feminism & Psychology* 25, no. 1 (2015): 11–17

52 Xiaoyan, "Whose Equality First? Some Observations on Gender and Sexuality Movements in China," *Queer Lala Times Anthology*, 1 (2014): 40–42.

53 Lucetta Kam, *Shanghai Lalas: Female Tongzhi Communities and Politics in Urban China* (Hong Kong: Hong Kong University Press, 2012).

54 Liu, Huang, and Ma, "Young Activists, New Movements," 15.

55 More information can be found in the documentary *The VaChina Monologues* (directed by Fan Popo, 2013).

56 Datu, "Join the Rights Feminism Movement as Straight Women, and Come Out as Queer Women," *Queer Lala Times Anthology*, 1 (2014): 64.

57 Quoted in Xiaoyan, "Whose Equality First?," 42.

58 Anonymous, personal communication, January 4, 2016.

59 Marjorie Garber, *Vested Interests: Cross-Dressing and Cultural Anxiety* (New York: Routledge, 1992).

60 Gaylyn Studlar, *This Mad Masquerade: Stardom and Masculinity in the Jazz Age* (New York: Columbia University Press, 1996); Urszula Chowaniec, Ursula Phillips, and Marja Rytkönen, eds., *Masquerade and Femininity: Essays on Russian and Polish Women Writers* (Cambridge: Cambridge Scholars Publishing, 2008).

61 Kathleen Woodward, "Youthfulness as a Masquerade," *Discourse* 11, no. 1 (Fall–Winter 1988): 125.

62 Thy Phu, *Picturing Model Citizens: Civility in Asian American Visual Culture* (Philadelphia: Temple University Press, 2011), 141.

63 Guerrilla Girls, Inc., "Guerrilla Girls Bare All," Archive.org, Guerrilla Girls, 1995, accessed April 15, 2021, www.web.archive.org.

64 Hanna Sophia Hörl, "Guerilla Girls Artivism: The Mixed Blessing of 'MASK-ulinity' and the Death of the Artist" in *Where My Girls At? Writings on Contemporary Feminist Art*, ed. Megan Bosence, Sakina Shakil Gröppmaier, Bärbel Harju, and Amelie Starke (München: University Library of Ludwig-Maximilians-Universität, 2021), 34.

65 Hörl, "Guerilla Girls Artivism," 31.

66 Rosi Braidotti, "Punk Women and Riot Grrls," *Performance Philosophy* 1 (2015): 249.

67 Braidotti, "Punk Women and Riot Grrls," 249.

68 Anonymous, personal communication, November 21, 2021.

69 Meili Xiao, member of YRFAS, personal communication, January 5, 2016.

70 Pin Lü, "Strive for Mainstream and Keep the Alternative," 2014, accessed June 20, 2016, www.nandu.com.

71 King, Pan, and Roberts, "How Censorship in China Allows," 326–43.

72 Jun Li, personal communication, January 10, 2016.

73 Ching Kwan Lee and You-Tien Hsing, "Social Activism in China: Agency and Possibility," in *Reclaiming Chinese Society: The New Social Activism*, ed. You-Tien Hsing and Ching Kwan Lee (Oxon, UK: Routledge, 2010), 1–13.

74 Lee and Hsing, "Social Activism in China," 6.

75 Lee and Hsing, "Social Activism in China," 9.

76 Samson Yuen, "Friend or Foe? The Diminishing Space of China's Civil Society," *China Perspectives* 3 (2015): 51.

77 Fengshi Wu and Kin-man Chan, "Graduated Control and Beyond: The Evolving Government-NGO Relations," *China Perspectives* 3 (2012): 9–17.

78 Clothey et al., "A Voice for the Voiceless," 858–74; Marielle S. Gleiss, "Speaking Up for the Suffering (Br)other: Weibo Activism, Discursive Struggles, and Minimal Politics in China," *Media, Culture & Society* 37, no. 4 (February 2015): 513–29.

79 Fan Yang, "Rethinking China's Internet Censorship: The Practice of Recoding and the Politics of Visibility," *New Media & Society* 18, no. 7 (October 2014): 1–18.

80 Wei Wei, "Street, Behavior, Art: Advocating Gender Rights and the Innovation of a Social Movement Repertoire," *Chinese Journal of Sociology* 1, no. 2 (May 2015): 279–304.

81 Thomas Poell, Jeroen Kloet, and Guohua Zeng, "Will the Real Weibo Please Stand Up? Chinese Online Contention and Actor-Network Theory," *Chinese Journal of Communication* 7, no. 1 (2014): 1–18; Yang Liu, "Tweeting, Re-Tweeting, and Commenting: Microblogging and Social Movements in China," *Asian Journal of Communication* 25, no. 6 (2015): 567–83.

82 For more details of the different posts, see Ling Han and Chengpang Lee, "Nudity, Feminists, and Chinese Online Censorship: A Case Study on the Anti-Domestic Violence Campaign on SinaWeibo," *China Information* 33, no. 3 (2019): 274–93.

83 Katrien Jacobs, *People's Pornography: Sex and Surveillance on the Chinese Internet* (Bristol, UK: Intellect, 2012).

84 Katrien Jacobs, "Disorderly Conduct: Feminist Nudity in Chinese Protest Movements," *Sexualities* 19, no. 7 (2016): 823.

85 Yangzi Sima, "Grassroots Environmental Activism and the Internet: Constructing a Green Public Sphere in China," *Asian Studies Review* 35, no. 4 (December 2011): 477–97.

86 Adrian Rauchfleisch and Mike S. Schäfer, "Multiple Public Spheres of Weibo: A Typology of Forms and Potentials of Online Public Spheres in China," *Information, Communication & Society* 18, no. 2 (2015): 151.

87 Marina Svensson, "Voice, Power and Connectivity in China's Microblogosphere: Digital Divides on SinaWeibo," *China Information* 28, no. 2 (July 2014): 168–88.

88 Fenton and Barassi, "Alternative Media," 179–96.

89 Fenton and Barassi, "Alternative Media," 191.

90 Fenton and Barassi, "Alternative Media," 191.

91 Wallis, "Gender and China's Online Censorship Protest Culture," 223–38.

92 Cao Jin, Xu Jing, and Huang Aohan, "New Media, New Rhetoric and the Relationship between Gender Politics and Class in China in Transition: The Case of 'Green Tea Bitch,'" *Journalism Bimonthly* 130, no. 2 (2015): 50–59.

93 Sara Liao, "'#IAmGay# What About You?': Storytelling, Discursive Politics, and the Affective Dimension of Social Media Activism against Censorship in China," *International Journal of Communication* 13 (2019): 2314–33.

94 Liao, "#IAmGay#," 2324.

95 Zhongxuan Lin and Liu Yang, "Individual and Collective Empowerment: Women's Voices in the #MeToo Movement in China," *Asian Journal of Women's Studies* 25, no. 1 (2019): 117–31.

96 Paolo Gerbaudo, *The Mask and the Flag: Populism, Citizenism, and Global Protest* (Oxford: Oxford University Press, 2017), 4.

97 Gerbaudo, *The Mask and the Flag*, 4.

2. PERFORMATIVE RIGHTS

1 See "Preface," *Women's Voice* 1 (September 2009): 1. Up till 2015, *Women's Voice* had published 150 issues.

2 "Connecting New Communities, Joining Social Transformation: Re-thinking Feminist Voices," *Women's Voice* 99 (October 2011): 1–7.

3 Howard Tumber and Silvio Waisbord, eds., *The Routledge Companion to Media and Human Rights* (London: Routledge, 2018).

4 Bonnie J. Dow and Julia T. Wood, "Repeating History and Learning from It: What Can Slut Walks Teach Us About Feminism?" *Women's Studies in Communication* 37, no. 1 (2014): 22–43; Tracy Everbach, "Women's (Mis)Representation in News Media," in *Media Disparity: A Gender Battleground*, ed. Cory L. Armstrong (Lanham, MD: Lexington Books, 2013), 15–26; and Barbara M. Freeman, *Beyond*

Bylines: Media Workers and Women's Rights in Canada (Kitchener-Waterloo, ON: Wilfrid Laurier University Press, 2011).

5 Barbara Barnett, "Dividing Women: The Framing of Trafficking for Sexual Exploitation in Magazines," *Feminist Media Studies* 16, no. 2 (2016): 205–22; Lisa M. Cuklanz, "Mass Media Representation of Gendered Violence," in *The Routledge Companion to Media and Gender*, ed. Cynthia Carter, Linda Steiner, and Lisa Mclaughlin (Oxon, UK: Routledge, 2014), 32–41; and Meghan R. Sobel, "Confronting Sex Trafficking: Gender Depictions in Newspaper Coverage from the Former Soviet Republics and the Baltic States," *European Journal of Communication* 31, no. 2 (2016): 152–68.

6 Anne Johnston, Barbara Friedman, and Meghan Sobel, "Framing an Emerging Issue: How U.S. Print and Broadcast News Media Covered Sex Trafficking, 2008–2012," *Journal of Human Trafficking* 1, no. 3 (2015): 235–54.

7 Thomas Chase, "Problems of Publicity: Online Activism and Discussion of Same-Sex Sexuality in South Korea and China," *Asian Studies Review* 36, no. 2 (2012): 151–70; Lynette J. Chua, "Negotiating Social Norms and Relations in the Micro-mobilization of Human Rights: The Case of Burmese Lesbian Activism," *Law and Social Inquiry* 41, no. 3 (2016): 643–69; and Elisabeth Jay Friedman, "Lesbians in (Cyber)Space: The Politics of the Internet in Latin American On- and Off-Line Communities," *Media, Culture & Society* 29, no. 5 (2007): 790–811.

8 Youngshik D. Bong, "The Gay Rights Movement in Democratizing Korea," *Korea Studies* 32 (2008): 86–103; Sonia Corrêa, Horacio Sívori, and Bruno Zilli, "Internet Regulation and Sexual Politics in Brazil," *Development* 55, no. 2 (2012): 213–18.

9 Henriette Gunkel, "Some Reflections on Postcolonial Homophobia, Local Interventions, and LGBTI Solidarity Online: The Politics of Global Petitions," *African Studies Review*, 56, no. 2 (2013): 67–81.

10 Judith Butler, *Gender Trouble: Feminism and the Subversion of Identity* (New York: Routledge, 2011).

11 Butler, *Gender Trouble*, 174–175.

12 Butler, *Gender Trouble*, 177.

13 Butler, *Gender Trouble*, 177.

14 Marina Svensson, *Debating Human Rights in China* (Lanham, MD: Rowman & Littlefield Publishers, 2002), 239.

15 Svensson, *Debating Human Rights in China*, 266.

16 China ratified ICESCR in 2001 and has not yet ratified ICCPR.

17 Hualing Fu and Richard Cullen, "*Weiquan* (Rights Protection) Lawyering in an Authoritarian State: Building a Culture of Public-interest Lawyering," *China Journal* 59 (2008): 111–27.

18 Li Xiaojiang, "Human Progress and Women's Emancipation," *Studies on Marxism* 1, no. 2 (1983): 142–66.

19 Li, "Human Progress and Women's Liberation," 165.

20 Min, *Translation and Travelling Theory*, 42–44.

21 Shih, *Visuality and Identity: Sinophone Articulations across the Pacific. Vol. 2* (Berkeley: University of California Press, 2007), 2.

22 Shih, *Visuality and Identity*, 20.

23 Common Language, *LGBTI Rights: From Grassroots to UN* (Beijing: Common Language), 2016.

24 Jonathan Benney, "Rights Defence and the Virtual China," *Asian Studies Review* 31, no. 4 (2007): 435–46.

25 Benney, "Rights Defence and the Virtual China," 437.

26 Benney, "Rights Defence and the Virtual China," 437.

27 Randall Peerenboom, *China's Long March toward Rule of Law* (Cambridge: Cambridge University Press, 2002).

28 John Erni, *Law and Cultural Studies: A Critical Rearticulation of Human Rights* (London and New York: Routledge 2019), 247.

29 Erni, *Law and Cultural Studies*, 247.

30 Anonymous, personal communication, January 8, 2019.

31 Aili Mari Tripp, "The Evolution of Transnational Feminisms," in *Global Feminism: Transnational Women's Activism, Organizing, and Human Rights*, ed. Myra Marx Ferree and Aili Mari Tripp (New York: New York University Press, 2006): 51–75.

32 Tripp, "The Evolution of Transnational Feminisms," 65.

33 UNDP China has participated in the release of reports such as *Being LGBTI in China: A National Survey on Social Attitudes towards Sexual Orientation, Gender Identity and Gender Expression* (2016) and *Legal Gender Recognition in China: A Legal and Policy Review* (2018).

34 For more, see "Law of the People's Republic of China on the Protection of Rights and Interests of Women," www.npc.gov.

35 Michele Mannoni, "Hefa Quanyi: More than a Problem of Translation: Linguistic Evidence of Lawfully Limited Rights in China," *International Journal for the Semiotics of Law* 32, no. 1 (2019): 29–46.

36 "Mission Statement," Beijing LGBT Center, accessed May 1, 2019, www .bjlgbtcenter.org.

37 "Mission Statement," PFLAG China, accessed May 1, 2019, www.pflag.org.

38 "Introduction to Family Equality Website," Family Equality Website, accessed May 1, 2019, http://pingjia.lgbt.

39 "Introduction to Family Equality Website."

40 Christina, personal communication, September 6, 2018.

41 Sebastian Veg, *Minjian: The Rise of China's Grassroots Intellectuals* (New York: Columbia University Press, 2019), 243.

42 Sally Engle Merry, *Human Rights and Gender Violence: Translating International Law into Local Justice* (Chicago: University of Chicago Press, 2006).

43 Peggy Levitt and Sally Merry, "Vernacularization on the Ground: Local Uses of Global Women's Rights in Peru, China, India and the United States," *Global Networks* 9, no. 4 (2009): 447.

44 Meng Liu, Yanhong Hu, and Minli Liao, "Travelling Theory in China: Contextualization, Compromise and Combination," *Global Networks* 9, no. 4 (2009): 529–53.

45 Levitt and Merry, "Vernacularization on the Ground," 457.

46 Levitt and Merry, "Vernacularization on the Ground," 457.

47 Liu, Hu, and Liao, "Travelling Theory in China," 537.

48 Liu, Hu, and Liao, "Travelling Theory in China," 540.

49 Liu, Hu, and Liao, "Travelling Theory in China," 549.

50 Timothy Hildebrandt, *Social Organizations and the Authoritarian State in China* (Cambridge: Cambridge University Press, 2013), 2.

51 Lynette J. Chua, *Mobilizing Gay Singapore: Rights and Resistance in an Authoritarian State* (Singapore: NUS Press, 2014), 5.

52 Benney, "Rights Defence and the Virtual China," 437.

53 Fu and Cullen, "*Weiquan* (Rights Protection) Lawyering," 112.

54 Jinyan Zeng, *Feminism and Genesis of the Citizen Intelligentsia in China* (Hong Kong: CITYU HK Press, 2016): 202–03.

55 See the brochure for China Women's Film Festival, 2015.

56 The State Administration of Press, Publication, Radio, Film, and Television was renamed the National Radio and Television Administration in 2018.

57 Young, personal communication, November 12, 2019.

3. QUEER BECOMING

Parts of chapter 3 have been adapted from Jia Tan, "Aesthetics of Queer Becoming: *Comrade Yue* and Chinese Community-Based Documentaries Online," *Critical Studies in Media Communication* 33, no. 1 (2016): 38–52.

1 For more information, see "Digital Storytelling Workshop," http://blog.sina.com.

2 Matthew David Johnson, Keith B. Wagner, Kiki Tianqi Yu, and Luke Vulpiani, eds., *China's iGeneration: Cinema and Moving Image Culture for the Twenty-First Century* (New York and London: Bloomsbury Academic), 1.

3 Xinyu Lü, "Rethinking China's New Documentary Movement: Engagement with the Social," in *The New Chinese Documentary Movement: For the Public Record*, ed. Chris Berry, Xinyu Lü, and Lisa Rofel (Hong Kong: Hong Kong University Press, 2010), 16.

4 Xinyu Lü, *Documenting China: The New Documentary Movement in Contemporary China* (Beijing: Sanlian Shudian Chubanshe, 2003).

5 Zhen Zhang, ed., *The Urban Generation: Chinese Cinema and Society at the Turn of the Twenty-First Century* (Durham: Duke University Press, 2007).

6 Paola Voci, *China on Video: Smaller-Screen Realities* (Abingdon and New York: Routledge, 2010).

7 Chris Berry and Lisa Rofel, "Introduction," in *The New Chinese Documentary Movement: For the Public Record*, ed. Chris Berry, Xinyu Lü, and Lisa Rofel (Hong Kong: Hong Kong University Press, 2010), 4.

8 Johnson, Wagner, Yu, and Vulpiani, *China's iGeneration*, 4.

9 Yunxiang Yan, *The Individualization of Chinese Society* (London: Bloomsbury Academic, 2009).

10 Johnson, Wagner, Yu, and Vulpiani, *China's iGeneration*, 4–5.

11 Qi Wang, *Memory, Subjectivity and Independent Chinese Cinema* (Edinburgh: Edinburgh University Press, 2014), 3.

12 Hairong Yan, "Neoliberal Governmentality and Neohumanism: Organizing Suzhi/Value Flow through Labor Recruitment Networks," *Cultural Anthropology: Journal of the Society for Cultural Anthropology* 18, no. 4 (2003): 493–523; Lisa Rofel, *Desiring China: Experiments in Neoliberalism, Sexuality, and Public Culture* (Durham: Duke University Press, 2007).

13 David Harvey, *A Brief History of Neoliberalism* (Oxford: Oxford University Press, 2005).

14 Alexandra Juhasz, "Learning the Five Lessons of YouTube: After Trying to Teach There, I Don't Believe the Hype," *Cinema Journal* 48, no. 2 (2009): 145–50.

15 Jia Tan, "Neoliberalized Romantic Encounter: *If You Are the One* and the Gender Politics of Chinese Reality TV," *Router: A Journal of Cultural Studies* 20 (2015): 79–102.

16 Paul Arthur, "Essay Questions: From Alain Resnais to Michael Moore," *Film Comment* 39, no. 1 (2003): 58.

17 Michael Renov, *The Subject of Documentary* (Minneapolis: University of Minnesota Press, 2004), 214.

18 Hamid Naficy, *An Accented Cinema: Exilic and Diasporic Filmmaking* (Princeton, NJ: Princeton University Press, 2001).

19 See Shu-mei Shih, *Visuality and Identity: Sinophone Articulations across the Pacific. Vol. 2* (Berkeley: University of California Press, 2007), 9.

20 Howard Chiang, "(De)Provincializing China Queer historicism and Sinophone postcolonial critique," in *Queer Sinophone Cultures*, ed. Howard Chiang and Ari Larissa Heinrich (New York: Routledge, 2013), 36.

21 Ari Larissa Heinrich, "'A Volatile Alliance': Queer Sinophone Synergies across Literature, Film, and Culture," in *Queer Sinophone Cultures*, ed. Chiang and Heinrich, 4.

22 Howard Chiang and Alvin K. Wong, eds., *Keywords in Queer Sinophone Studies* (New York: Routledge, 2020), 3.

23 Audrey Yue, "Mobile Intimacies in the Queer Sinophone Films of Cui Zi'en," *Journal of Chinese Cinemas* 6, no. 1 (2012): 105.

24 Lisa Rofel, *Desiring China: Experiments in Neoliberalism, Sexuality, and Public Culture* (Durham: Duke University Press, 2007).

25 For more, see "Advice Section: Queer Theory," www.aibai.com.

26 For more, see "Provisional Regulations concerning Appraising Obscene and Sexual Publications," https://chinacopyrightandmedia.wordpress.com.

27 See Helen Hok-Sze Leung, *Farewell My Concubine: A Queer Film Classic* (Vancouver: Arsenal Pulp Press, 2010).

28 Song Hwee Lim, *Celluloid Comrades: Representations of Male Homosexuality in Contemporary Chinese Cinemas* (Honolulu: University of Hawai'i Press, 2006).

29 Ling Yang and Hongwei Bao, "Queerly Intimate: Friends, Fans and Affective Communication in a Super Girl Fan Fiction Community," *Cultural Studies* 26, no. 6 (2012): 842; Haiqing Yu and Audrey Yue, "China's Super Girl Mobile Youth Cultures and New Sexualities," in *Youth, Media and Culture in the Asia Pacific Region*, ed. Usha Manchanda Rodrigues and Berlinda Smail (Newcastle, UK: Cambridge Scholars Publishing, 2008).

30 Luke Robinson, "Ethics, the Body and Digital Video," in *Independent Chinese Documentary: From the Studio to the Street* (Basingstoke, UK: Palgrave Macmillan, 2013), 103–29.

31 Shi-Yan Chao, *Queer Representations in Chinese-language Film and the Cultural Landscape* (Amsterdam: Amsterdam University Press, 2020).

32 Hongwei Bao. "The 'Queer Generation': Queer Community Documentary in Contemporary China," *Transnational Screens* 10, no. 3 (2019): 201–16.

33 Stijn Deklerck and Xiaogang Wei, "Queer Online Media and the Building of China's LGBT Community," in *Queer/Tongzhi China: New Perspectives on Research, Activism and Media Culture*, ed. Elisabeth L. Engebretsen and William F. Schroeder (Copenhagen: NIAS Press, 2015), 18–34.

34 For an in-depth exploration of the digital filmmaking in Pink Space, see Hongwei Bao, "Queering International Development: The 'Pleasure Principle' in the Participatory Video *The Lucky One*," *Feminist Media Studies* 20, no. 4 (2020): 530–47.

35 For more online videos released by Queer Comrades, see www.queercomrades.com.

36 Deklerck and Wei, "Queer Online Media."

37 For more, see Ben Child, "Film-Maker Sues Chinese Censors over 'Ban' on Gay-Themed Movie," www.theguardian.com.

38 Gareth Shaw and Xiaoling Zhang, "Cyberspace and Gay Rights in a Digital China: Queer Documentary Filmmaking under State Censorship," *China Information* 32, no. 2 (2018): 270–92.

39 Faye Ginsburg, Lila Abu-Lughod, and Brian Larkin, eds., *Media World: Anthropology on New Terrain* (Berkeley: University of California Press, 2002), 7.

40 Adrienne Rich, "Compulsory Heterosexuality and Lesbian Existence," *Signs: Journal of Women in Culture and Society* 5 (1980): 631–60; Michael Warner, "Introduction: Fear of a Queer Planet," *Social Text* 9, no. 4 (1991): 3–17.

41 Loretta W. Ho, "The Gay Space in Chinese Cyberspace: Self-Censorship, Commercialisation and Misrepresentation," in *Gay and Lesbian Subculture in Urban China* (New York: Routledge, 2010), 99–117.

42 Keeling, "Queer OS," 153.

43 Keeling, "Queer OS," 153.

4. NETWORKING ASIA PACIFIC

An earlier version of chapter 4 has appeared as Jia Tan, "Networking Asia Pacific: Queer Film Festivals and the Spatiotemporal Politics of Inter-Referencing," *Inter-Asia Cultural Studies* 20, no. 2 (2019): 204–19.

1 Dipesh Chakrabarty, *Provincializing Europe: Postcolonial Thought and Historical Difference* (Princeton: Princeton University Press, 2000), 28.

2 Kuan-Hsing Chen, *Asia as Method: Toward Deimperialization* (Durham, NC: Duke University Press, 2010), xv.

3 Chua, "Inter-Asia Referencing and Shifting Frames of Comparison," 67–80.

4 Aihwa Ong, "Introduction: Worlding Cities, or the Art of Being Global," in *Worlding Cities: Asian Experiments and the Art of Being Global*, ed. Ananya Roy and Aihwa Ong (West Sussex, UK: Blackwell, 2011), 17.

5 Chua Beng Huat, "Inter-Asia Referencing and Shifting Frames of Comparison," in *The Social Sciences in the Asian Century*, ed. Carol Johnson, Vera Mackie, and Tessa Morris-Suzuki (Acton, AU: Australian National University Press, 2015), 68.

6 Chua, "Inter-Asia Referencing and Shifting Frames of Comparison," 78; Koichi Iwabuchi, "De-Westernisation, Inter-Asian Referencing and Beyond," *European Journal of Cultural Studies* 17, no. 1 (2014): 44–57.

7 Lisa Yoneyama, "Toward a Decolonial Genealogy of the Transpacific," *American Quarterly* 69, no. 3 (2017): 472.

8 Marijke de Valck and Skadi Loist, "Film Festival Studies: An Overview of a Burgeoning Field," in *Film Festival Yearbook 1: The Festival Circuit*, ed. Dina Lordanova and Ragan Rhyne (St Andrews, UK: St. Andrews Film Studies, 2009), 179–215.

9 de Valck and Loist, "Film Festival Studies," 179.

10 Aaron Krach, "Unlocking the Secrets of the Screening Committee," *Independent Film & Video Monthly*, April 1, 2003, http://independent-magazine.org; Patricia Thomson, "Clutterbusters: Programmers at Five Leading Festivals Expound on Heady Process of Selecting Films," *Variety*, August 18, 2003, http://variety.com.

11 Gideon Bachmann, "Insight into the Growing Festival Influence: Fest Vet Discusses 'Wholesale' and 'Retail' Events," *Variety*, August 28, 2000, http://variety.com; Daryl Chin, and Larry Qualls, "Open Circuits, Closed Markets: Festivals and Expositions of Film and Video," *PAJ: A Journal of Performance and Art* 23, no. 1 (2001): 33–47; Daryl Chin and Larry Qualls, "Three Blind Mice: Fairs, Festivals, Expositions," *PAJ: A Journal of Performance and Art* 26, no. 3 (2004): 61–71.

12 Owen Evans, "Border Exchanges: The Role of the European Film Festival," *Journal of Contemporary European Studies* 15, no. 1 (2007): 23–33; Julian Stringer, "Regarding Film Festivals" (PhD diss. Indiana University, 2003).

13 Bill Nichols, "Discovering Form, Inferring Meaning: New Cinemas and the Film Festival Circuit," *Film Quarterly* 47, no. 3 (1994): 16–30; Julian Stringer, "Genre Films and Festival Communities: Lessons from Nottingham, 1991–2000," *Film International* 6, no. 4 (2008): 53–60.

14 Soo Jeong Ahn, "Re-Imagining the Past: Programming South Korean Retrospectives at the Pusan International Film Festival," *Film International* 6, no. 4 (2008): 24–33; Thomas Elsaesser, "Film Festival Networks: The New Topographies of Cinema in Europe," in *European Cinema: Face to Face with Hollywood* (Amsterdam: Amsterdam University Press, 2005), 82–107; Julian Stringer, "Global Cities and International Film Festival Economy," in *Cinema and the City: Film and Ur-*

ban Societies in a Global Context, ed. Mark Shiel and Tony Fitzmaurice (Oxford: Blackwell, 2001), 134–44.

15 Marijke de Valck, *Film Festivals: From European Geopolitics to Global Cinephilia* (Amsterdam: Amsterdam University Press, 2007).

16 Elsaesser, "Film Festival Networks"; de Valck, *Film Festivals*.

17 de Valck, *Film Festivals*, 15.

18 Manuel Castells, *The Rise of the Network Society* (Cambridge, MA: Blackwell Publishers, 2002).

19 Saskia Sassen, *The Global City: New York, London, Tokyo* (Princeton: Princeton University Press, 2001).

20 de Valck, *Film Festivals*, 214.

21 de Valck, *Film Festivals*, 208.

22 As suggested by the Mardi Gras Film Festival in Sydney, there have been lesbian and gay film festivals in Sydney since 1978. For more, see https://queerscreen.org.

23 Among them are the establishments of Beijing Queer Film Festival in 2001, Q!Film Festival in Jakarta in 2002, Abhimani Queer Film Festival in Colombo in 2005, Kansai Queer Film Festival in Kansai in 2005, ShanghaiPRIDE Film Festival in 2009, KASHISH Mumbai International Queer Film Festival in 2010. This website on queer film festival studies provides an interactive global map of queer film festivals: http://reframe.sussex.ac.uk.

24 Stephen Kent Jusick, "Gay Art Guerrillas: Interview with Jim Hubbard and Sarah Schulman," in *That's Revolting! Queer Strategies for Resisting Assimilation*, ed. Matt Bernstein Sycamore (Brooklyn: Soft Skull Press, 2004), 39–58; Susan Stryker, "A Cinema of One's Own: A Brief History of the San Francisco International Lesbian & Gay Film Festival," in *The Ultimate Guide to Lesbian & Gay Film and Video*, ed. Jenni Olson (New York: Serpent's Tail, 1996), 364–70.

25 de Valck, *Film Festivals*.

26 Sangjoon Lee, "Creating an Anti-Communist Motion Picture Producers' Network in Asia: The Asia Foundation, Asia Pictures, and the Korean Motion Picture Cultural Association," *Historical Journal of Film, Radio and Television* 37, no. 3 (2017): 517–38.

27 Network of Asian Women's Film Festival, "NAWFF Award Ceremony Held in Taiwan," *Taiwan Today*, October 16, 2013, https://taiwantoday.tw/. For more information, see the website of the Taiwan Women's Film Association, which organizes the Women Make Waves Film Festival: www.wmw.org.tw.

28 Louise Nealson, "Media Release: Queer Screen's Mardi Gras Film Festival Turns the Spotlight on Asia; Hosting the Asia Pacific Queer Film Festival Alliance," Mardi Gras Film Festival, January 23, 2017, PDF file, https://queerscreen.org.au.

29 Asian Film Festivals, "Asian Pacific LGBTQ Short Films Present at the Mardi Gras Film Festival 2017," Asian Film Festivals, February 18, 2017, https://asianfilmfestivals.com.

30 James Marsh, "Five Hong Kong Film Festivals to Get Excited about in September," *South China Morning Post*, September 5, 2017, www.scmp.com.

31 Jen Armstrong, "The 29th Annual Honolulu Rainbow Film Festival Presented by Bank of Hawaiʻi; All-Access Festival Passes on Sale April 1ˢᵗ," The Honolulu Rainbow Film Festival, March 22, 2018, PDF file, https://hglcf.org/.

32 Honolulu Rainbow Film Festival, "2018 Honolulu Rainbow Film Festival Program Guide," Honolulu Rainbow Film Festival, 2018, PDF file, https://hglcf.org/.

33 The Daily Eye Team, "Indian Film 'Any Other Day' Wins the Asia Pacific Award for Best Queer Film," Daily Eye, October 26, 2017, https://thedailyeye.info/.

34 Helen Hok-Sze Leung and Audrey Yue, "Queer Asia as Method: Reorienting the Borders of Queer Knowledge," paper presented at the 130th MLA Annual Convention, Vancouver, January 8–11, 2015. See also Audrey Yue, "Trans-Singapore: Some Notes towards Queer Asia as Method," Inter-Asia Cultural Studies 18, no. 1 (2017): 21.

35 Armstrong, "The 29th Annual Honolulu Rainbow Film Festival."

36 Dean Hamer, Board of Directors, Honolulu Gay & Lesbian Cultural Foundation, personal communication, October 25, 2018.

37 Hamer, personal communication.

38 Christine Kim and Helen Hok-Sze Leung, "The Minor Transpacific: A Round-Table Discussion," BC Studies: The British Columbian Quarterly 198 (2018): 13.

39 Viet Thanh Nguyen and Janet Hoskins, "Introduction: Transpacific Studies: Critical Perspectives on an Emerging Field," in Transpacific Studies: Framing an Emerging Field, ed. Janet Hoskins and Viet Thanh Nguyen (Honolulu: University of Hawaiʻi Press, 2014), 3.

40 Rob Wilson and Arif Dirlik, eds., Asia/Pacific as Space of Cultural Production (Durham, NC: Duke University Press, 1995).

41 Inderpal Grewal and Caren Kaplan, eds., Scattered Hegemonies: Postmodernity and Transnational Feminist Practices (Minneapolis: University of Minnesota Press, 1994).

42 Chua Beng Huat and Koichi Iwabuchi, eds., East Asian Pop Culture: Analysing the Korean Wave (Hong Kong: Hong Kong University Press, 2008).

43 Melani Budianta, "Shifting the Geographies of Knowledge: The Unfinished Project of Inter-Asia Cultural Studies," Inter-Asia Cultural Studies 11, no. 2 (2010): 174–77.

44 See Hee-Yeon Cho and Kuan-Hsing Chen, "Editorial Introduction: Bandung/Third Worldism," Inter-Asia Cultural Studies 6, no. 4 (2005): 473–75; Kuan-Hsing Chen, "Introduction: 'Bandung/Third World 60 Years'—in Memory of Professor Sam Moyo," Inter-Asia Cultural Studies 17, no. 1 (2016): 1–3.

45 Setsu Shigematsu and Keith L. Camacho, "Introduction: Militarized Currents, Decolonizing Futures," in Militarized Currents: Toward a Decolonized Future in Asia and the Pacific, ed. Setsu Shigematsu and Keith L. Camacho (Minneapolis: University of Minnesota Press, 2010), xv–xlviii.

46 Epeli Hauʻofa, "Our Sea of Islands," in We Are the Ocean: Selected Works (Honolulu: University of Hawaiʻi Press, 2008), 27–40.

47 Hauʻofa, "Our Sea of Islands."

48 Leo Ching, "Inter-Asia Cultural Studies and the Decolonial-Turn," *Inter-Asia Cultural Studies* 11, no. 2 (2010): 184–87.

49 Jia Tan, "Beijing Meets Hawai'i: Reflections on Ku'er, Indigeneity, and Queer Theory," *GLQ: A Journal of Lesbian and Gay Studies* 23, no. 1 (2017): 137–50.

50 Vernadette Vicuña Gonzalez, *Securing Paradise: Tourism and Militarism in Hawai'i and the Philippines* (Durham, NC: Duke University Press, 2013).

51 "Lady Eva," Frameline, 2017, www.frameline.org.

52 Louis Staples, "Organising a Trans Beauty Pageant in Conservative Tonga," *Dazed*, May 31, 2018, www.dazeddigital.com.

53 General regulations of and application form for submission of films to the 2015 the third China women's film festival, China Women's Film Festival, 2015, https://site.douban.com.

54 Asia-Pacific Queer Cinema and Cultural Forums, Taiwan International Queer Film Festival, October 27, 2017, www.tiqff.com.

55 Petrus Liu, *Queer Marxism in Two Chinas* (Durham, NC: Duke University Press, 2015), 164.

56 Stuart Richards, *The Queer Film Festival: Popcorn and Politics* (New York: Palgrave Macmillan, 2016), 144.

57 Richards, *The Queer Film Festival*, 201, 205.

58 Joceline Andersen, "From the Ground Up: Transforming the Inside Out LGBT Film and Video Festival of Toronto," *Canadian Journal of Film Studies* 21, no. 1 (2012): 38–57; Stuart Richards, "Frameline's Conservative Hoax: Smashing Frameline's Homonormative Image to Reveal a Socially Empowering Organisation," *AntiTHESIS: A Postgraduate Journal of Interdisciplinary Studies* 22 (2012): 123–39.

59 Jeongmin Kim, "Queer Cultural Movements and Local Counterpublics of Sexuality: A Case of Seoul Queer Films and Videos Festival," *Inter-Asia Cultural Studies* 8, no. 4 (2007): 617–33; Ger Zielinski, "On the Production of Heterotopia, and Other Spaces, in and around Lesbian and Gay Film Festivals," *Jump Cut: A Review of Contemporary Media* 54 (2012), www.ejumpcut.org.

60 Ma Ran, "Celebrating the International, Disremembering Shanghai: The Curious Case of the Shanghai International Film Festival," *Culture Unbound: Journal of Current Cultural Research* 4 (2012): 147–68; Dina Iordanova, "East Asia and Film Festivals: Transnational Clusters for Creativity and Commerce," in *Film Festival Yearbook 3: Film Festivals and East Asia*, ed. Dina Iordanova and Ruby Cheung (St Andrews, UK: St Andrews Film Studies, 2011), 1–33.

61 Chris Berry, "10 Years Young: The Shanghai International Film Festival," *Senses of Cinema* 45 (2007), http://sensesofcinema.com.

62 Ma, "Celebrating the International, Disremembering Shanghai."

63 Berry, "10 Years Young."

64 Ruby Cheung, "East Asian Film Festivals: Film Markets," in *Film Festival Yearbook 3: Film Festivals and East Asia*, ed. Dina Iordanova and Ruby Cheung (St Andrews, UK: St Andrews Film Studies, 2011), 40–61.

65 Ting, organizer of Shanghai Queer Film Festival and SHPFF in 2017, personal communication, June 8, 2018.

66 Abé Mark Nornes, "Bulldozers, Bibles and Very Sharp Knives: The Chinese Independent Documentary Scene. Reports from the Thriving Festivals in Kunming and Songzhuang, China," *Film Quarterly* 63, no. 1 (2009): 50–55; Chris Berry, "When Is a Film Festival Not a Festival? The 6th China Independent Film Festival," *Senses of Cinema* 53 (2009), http://sensesofcinema.com; Ma Ran, "Regarding the Grassroots Chinese Independent Film Festivals: Modes of Multiplicity and Abnormal Film Networking," in *China's iGeneration: Cinema and Moving Image Culture for the Twenty-First Century*, ed. Matthew D. Johnson, Keith B. Wagner, Tianqi Yu, and Luke Vulpiani (New York: Bloomsbury Academic, 2014), 235–54.

67 Luke Robinson and Jenny Chio, "Making Space for Chinese Independent Documentary: The Case of Yunfest 2011," *Journal of Chinese Cinemas* 7, no. 1 (2013): 21–40.

68 Ma, "Regarding the Grassroots Chinese Independent Film Festivals."

69 Berry, "When Is a Film Festival Not a Festival?"

70 Lydia Wu, "How Does It Survive? The 10th Beijing Independent Film Festival," *Senses of Cinema* 68 (2013), http://sensesofcinema.com; Shelly Kraicer, "Shelly on Film: Fall Festival Report, Part One: Keeping Independence in Beijing," *dGenerate Films*, December 6, 2011, http://dgeneratefilms.com.

71 Elisabeth L. Engebretsen, "Queer 'Guerrilla' Activism in China: Reflections on the Tenth-Anniversary Beijing Queer Film Festival 2011," *Trikster*, October 10, 2011, http://trikster.net; Cui Zi'en, "The Communist International of Queer Film," *Positions: East Asia Cultures Critique* 18, no. 2 (2010): 417–23; Kraicer, "Shelly on Film."

72 Hongwei Bao, "Enlightenment Space, Affective Space: Travelling Queer Film Festival in China," in *Gender, Mobility and Citizenship in Asia*, ed. Mikako Iwatake (Helsinki: Renvall Institute Publications, 2010), 174–205; Wu, "How Does It Survive?"

73 Hongwei Bao, "Queer as Catachresis: The Beijing Queer Film Festival in Cultural Translation," in *Chinese Film Festivals: Sites of Translation*, ed. Chris Berry and Luke Robinson (London: Palgrave Macmillan, 2017), 95.

74 Antoine Damiens, *LGBTQ Film Festivals: Curating Queerness* (Amsterdam: Amsterdam University Press, 2020).

75 Fan Popo, personal communication, April 26, 2017.

76 Sandro Mezzadra and Brett Neilson, *Border as Method, Or, the Multiplication of Labor* (Durham, NC: Duke University Press, 2013), 59.

77 Mezzadra and Neilson, *Border as Method*, 58–59.

78 Hongwei Bao, "The Queer Global South: Transnational Video Activism Between China and Africa," *Global Media and China* 5, no. 3 (2020): 294–318.

79 Yue, "Trans-Singapore," 21.

80 Chua, "Inter-Asia Referencing and Shifting Frames of Comparison," 78.

5. PLATFORM PRESENTISM

1 The app The L was rebranded as Rela in 2016 and changed its name back to The L in 2021. In this chapter, I use The L to refer to the app and the company in a general sense.

2 Paola Voci, *China on Video: Smaller-Screen Realities* (London and New York: Routledge, 2010), 77.

3 Voci, *China on Video*, 78.

4 Stuart Cunningham, David Craig, and Jon Silver, "YouTube, Multichannel Networks and the Accelerated Evolution of the New Screen Ecology," *Convergence* 22, no. 4 (2016): 376–91, http://doi.org/10.1177/1354856516641620.

5 Lisa Duggan, "The New Homonormativity: The Sexual Politics of Neoliberalism," in *Materializing Democracy: Toward a Revitalized Cultural Politics*, ed. Russ Castronovo and Dana Nelson (Durham, NC: Duke University Press, 2002), 175–94.

6 *Pin tai hua* is a popular digital business discourse, as evident in books on platformization, such as Wenqi Duan, *Strategic Studies of the Platformization of Professional Market and Digital Business Convergence* (Beijing: China Social Science Chubanshe, 2014).

7 Martin Kenney and John Zysman, "The Rise of the Platform Economy," *Issues in Science and Technology* 32, no. 3 (2016).

8 Paul Langley and Andrew Leyshon, "Platform Capitalism: The Intermediation and Capitalization of Digital Economic Circulation," *Finance and Society* 3, no. 1 (2017): 11–31.

9 Yu Hong, *Networking China: The Digital Transformation of the Chinese Economy* (Urbana: University of Illinois Press, 2017).

10 Lianrui Jia and Dwayne Winseck, "The Political Economy of Chinese Internet Companies: Financialization, Concentration, and Capitalization," *International Communication Gazette* 80, no. 1 (2018): 30–59, http://doi.org/10.1177/1748048517742783.

11 Elaine Jing Zhao, "The Bumpy Road towards Network Convergence in China: The Case of Over-the-Top Streaming Services," *Global Media and China* 2, no. 1 (2017): 28–42, http://doi.org/10.1177/2059436416688698.

12 Michael Keane, "Disconnecting, Connecting, and Reconnecting: How Chinese Television Found Its Way Out of the Box," *International Journal of Communication* 10 (2016): 5426–43, http://ijoc.org.

13 Jie Gu, "From Divergence to Convergence: Institutionalization of Copyright and the Decline of Online Video Piracy in China," *International Communication Gazette* 80, no. 1 (2018): 60–86, http://doi.org/10.1177/1748048517742785.

14 Audrey Yue, "'We're the Gay Company, As Gay As It Gets': The Social Enterprise of Fridae," in *Queer Singapore: Illiberal Citizenship and Mediated Cultures*, edited by Audrey Yue and Jun Zubillaga-Pow (Hong Kong: Hong Kong University Press, 2012), 212.

15 Denise Tse-Shang Tang, "All I Get Is an Emoji: Dating on Lesbian Mobile Phone App Butterfly," *Media, Culture & Society* 39, no. 6 (2017): 816–832; Tingting Liu, "LESDO: Emerging Digital Infrastructures of Community-Based Care for Female Queer Subjects," *Feminist Media Studies* 17, no. 2 (2017): 301–305.

16 Lik Sam Chan, *The Politics of Dating Apps: Gender, Sexuality, and Emergent Publics in Urban China* (Cambridge, MA: MIT Press, 2021).

17 Sandra Harding, *The Science Question in Feminism* (New York: Cornell University Press, 1986); Judy Wajcman, "Feminist Theories of Technology," *Cambridge Journal of Economics* 34, no. 1 (2009): 143–52, http://doi.org/10.1093/cje/ben057.

18 Wendy Hui Kyong Chun, "Introduction: Race and/as Technology; or, How to Do Things to Race," in *Camera Obscura*, 7–35; Tara McPherson, "Designing for Difference," *Differences* 25, no. 1 (2014): 177–88, http://doi.org/10.1215/10407391-2420039.

19 James Gleick, *Faster: The Acceleration of Just about Everything* (New York: Random House, 2000).

20 Robert Hassan, "Digital, Ethical, Political: Network Time and Common Responsibility," in *New Media and Society* (2017), http://doi.org/10.1177/1461444817726331.

21 Judy Wajcman, *Pressed for Time: The Acceleration of Life in Digital Capitalism* (Chicago: University of Chicago Press, 2015).

22 Wajcman, *Pressed for Time*, 35.

23 Gareth Shaw, and Xiaoling Zhang, "Cyberspace and Gay Rights in a Digital China: Queer Documentary Filmmaking under State Censorship," *China Information* (2017), http://doi.org/10.1177/0920203X17734134.

24 China Netcasting Services Association, "2016 Research Report on the Development of Online Video in China," 2016, accessed March 1, 2018, www.199it.com.

25 China Netcasting Services Association, "2016 Research Report."

26 For the long history of homoeroticism in Chinese film history, Hong Kong filmmaker Stanley Kwan's documentary *Yang ± Yin: Gender in Chinese Cinema* (1998) walks through the history of Chinese cinema through the eyes of the openly-gay film director.

27 Chris Berry and Lisa Rofel, "Introduction," in *The New Chinese Documentary Movement*, 3–14.

28 Luke Robinson, *Independent Chinese Documentary: From the Studio to the Street* (New York: Palgrave Macmillan, 2013).

29 Helen Hok-Sze Leung, "Homosexuality and Queer Aesthetics," in *A Companion to Chinese Cinema*, ed. Yingjin Zhang (Malden, MA: Wiley-Blackwell, 2012), 518–34.

30 Jia Tan, "Beijing Meets Hawai'i: Reflections on Kuer, Indigeneity, and Queer Theory," *GLQ: A Journal of Lesbian and Gay Studies* 23, no. 1 (2017).

31 Gareth Shaw and Xiaoling Zhang, "Cyberspace and Gay Rights in a Digital China: Queer Documentary Filmmaking under State Censorship," *China Information* (2017): 16, http://doi.org/10.1177/0920203X17734134.

32 For more about Butterfly, see Denise Tse-Shang Tang, "All I Get Is an Emoji: Dating on Lesbian Mobile Phone App Butterfly," *Media, Culture & Society* 39, no. 6 (2017): 816–32, https://doi.org/10.1177/0163443717693680.

33 José van Dijck, "Facebook as a Tool for Producing Sociality and Connectivity," *Television and New Media* 13, no. 2 (2012): 160–76, http://doi.org/10.1177/1527476411415291.

34 LESDO staff C, personal communication, November 2, 2017.

35 Elaine Jing Zhao, "Professionalization of Amateur Production in Online Screen Entertainment in China: Hopes, Frustrations, and Uncertainties," *International Journal of Communication* 10 (2016): 5444–62, http://ijoc.org/index.php/ijoc/article/view/5727/1834.

36 Mark Davis and Jian Xiao, "De-westernizing Platform Studies: History and Logics of Chinese and US Platforms," *International Journal of Communication* 15 (2021): 109.

37 China Netcasting Services, "The China Netcasting Services Association Announces the General Principles of Internet Audiovisual Programme Content Review," January 1, 2018, www.cnsa.cn.

38 Sarah Buckley, "China's High-Speed Sexual Revolution," *BBC News*, February 2016.

39 Fran Martin, *Backward Glances: Contemporary Chinese Cultures and the Female Homoerotic Imaginary* (Durham and London: Duke University Press, 2010).

40 Martin, *Backward Glances*, 7.

41 LESDO staff B, personal communication, November 2, 2017.

42 LESDO staff C, personal communication, November 2, 2017.

43 Harriet Evans, "Sexed Bodies, Sexualized Identities, and the Limits of Gender," *China Information* 22, no. 2 (2008): 361–86, http://doi.org/10.1177/0920203X08091550.

44 Jun Zhang and Peidong Sun, "'When Are You Going to Get Married?' Parental Matchmaking and Middle-Class Women in Contemporary Urban China," in *Wives, Husbands, and Lovers: Marriage and Sexuality in Hong Kong, Taiwan, and Urban China* (Stanford: Stanford University Press, 2014), 118–44.

45 LESDO staff A, personal communication, November 3, 2017.

46 LESDO staff A, personal communication, November 3, 2017.

47 Adrienne Rich, "Compulsory Heterosexuality and Lesbian Existence," *Signs: Journal of Women in Culture and Society* 5, no. 4 (1980): 631–60.

48 Laura Mulvey, "Visual Pleasure and Narrative Cinema," *Screen* 16, no. 3 (1975): 6–18.

49 Tingting Liu, "The Empowerment of Rural Migrant Lalas: Contending Queerness and Heteronormativity in China," *China Information* 33, no. 2 (2019): 165–184

50 Shan Juan, "'Pink Economy' Set to Soar as Companies Target LGBT Community," *China Daily*, December 1, 2016, www.chinadaily.com.cn.

51 Javier C. Hernández, "Building a Community, and an Empire, with a Gay Dating App in China," *New York Times*, December 16, 2016, www.nytimes.com.

52 LESDO staff A, personal communication, November 3, 2017.

53 "Innovation Park," interview with Rela, 2016, accessed March 1, 2018, www.ctoutiao.com.

54 José van Dijck, "Facebook as a Tool for Producing Sociality and Connectivity," *Television and New Media* 13, no. 2 (2012): 160–76, http://doi.org/10.1177/1527476411415291.

55 Ying-Chao Kao, "The Coloniality of Queer Theory: The Effects of 'Homonormativity' on Transnational Taiwan's Path to Equality," *Sexualities* (2021), https://doi:10.1177/13634607211047518.

56 Jennifer M. Kang, "Just Another Platform for Television? The Emerging Web Dramas as Digital Culture in South Korea," *Media, Culture & Society* 39, no. 5 (2017): 762–72, http://doi.org/10.1177/0163443717709442.

57 Pamela Robertson Wojcik, *The Apartment Plot: Urban Living in American Film and Popular Culture, 1945 to 1975* (Durham, NC: Duke University Press, 2010).

58 Wojcik, 42.

59 Wojcik, 40.

60 Lee Wallace, *Lesbianism, Cinema, Space: The Sexual Life of Apartments* (London and New York: Routledge, 2008).

61 "Chinese Lesbian Dating App Rela Shuts Down," *BBC*, May 30, 2017, www.bbc.com.

62 Alice Yan, "Why China's Gays and Lesbians Are Still Stuck in the Closet," *South China Morning Post*, 2017, accessed January 1, 2018, www.scmp.com.

63 Thomas Lamarre, "Platformativity: Media Studies, Area Studies," *Asiascape: Digital Asia* 4, no. 3 (2017): 285–305.

64 Nick Smicek, *Platform Capitalism* (Cambridge, UK: Polity Press, 2016).

65 Duggan, "The New Homonormativity."

66 LESDO staff C, personal communication, November 2, 2017.

67 Ge Zhang and Larissa Hjorth, "Live-Streaming, Games and Politics of Gender Performance: The Case of *Nüzhubo* in China," *Convergence: The International Journal of Research into New Media Technologies* (2017), http://doi.org/10.1177/1354856517738160.

CODA

1 Yun Zhou, "The 100 Days of Silencing Feminism," accessed August 9, 2021, https://theinitium.com.

2 Zhou, "The 100 Days of Silencing Feminism."

3 Braidotti, "Punk Women and Riot Grrls," 249.

4 For more on the #MeToo movement in China, see Zhongxuan Lin and Liu Yang, "Individual and Collective Empowerment: Women's Voices in the #MeToo Movement in China," *Asian Journal of Women's Studies* 25, no. 1 (2019): 117–131.

5 Kara Keeling, "Queer OS," *Cinema Journal* 53, no. 2 (2014): 153.

6 Tom Phillips, "China Passes Law Imposing Security Controls on Foreign NGOs," accessed August 9, 2020, www.theguardian.com.

7 Lin Song, "Straightly Chinese: The Emergence of Systemic Homophobia in China," *Contesting Chineseness: Ethnicity, Identity, and Nation in China and Southeast Asia*, ed. Chang-Yan Hoon and Ying-kit Chan (Singapore: Springer, 2021), 315.

8 For more information on the Chinese feminist activists who moved overseas, see "Rescuing the Ten-Year History of Chinese Feminist Movement," edited by Mimiyana, accessed August 9, 2021, www.wainao.me.

9 For more information, see Qi Ling and Sara Liao, "Intellectuals Debate #MeToo in China: Legitimizing Feminist Activism, Challenging Gendered Myths, and Reclaiming Feminism," *Journal of Communication* 70, no. 6 (2020): 895–916, https://doi.org/10.1093/joc/jqaa033.

10 "Nüquan ba," Baidu, accessed August 9, 2020, https://tieba.baidu.com.

11 Angela Xiao Wu and Yige Dong, "What Is Made-in-China Feminism(s)? Gender Discontent and Class Friction in Post-Socialist China," *Critical Asian Studies* 51, no. 4 (2019): 471–92, https://doi.org/10.1080/14672715.2019.1656538.

INDEX

Page numbers in *italics* indicate Figures

ABOUT THE AUTHOR

JIA TAN is Assistant Professor of Cultural Studies at the Chinese University of Hong Kong.